Thomas A. Giovanetti

Discus Fish

Aquatic Consultant: David Schleser
Aquatic Biologist, Dallas Aquarium

With 25 Color Photos
Illustrations by Michele Earle-Bridges

Consulting Editor: Matthew M. Vriends, PhD

BARRON'S

Cover Photos:
Inside front cover: A pair of turquoise discus, perhaps wondering if the aquarist is about to drop food in the aquarium. The dense growth of plants in the background is more attractive than any artificial background.
Inside back cover: Blue discus. The lower fish possesses the characteristic coloration of blue discus, whereas the yellow body of the upper fish is more reminiscent of green discus, though it lacks the latter's characteristic red spots.
Back cover: Above left, a turquoise x Heckel; above right, a blue discus; below left, green discus in a breeding installation; below right, a solid brilliant turquoise discus.

© Copyright 1991 by Barron's Educational Series, Inc.

All inquiries should be addressed to:
Barron's Educational Series, Inc.
250 Wireless Boulevard
Hauppauge, NY 11788

International Standard Book No. 0-8120-4669-2

Library of Congress Catalog Card No. 91-13946

Library of Congress Cataloging-in-Publication Data

Giovanetti, Thomas A.
　　Discus fish / Thomas A. Giovanetti ; consulting editor, Matthew M. Vriends; with color photos by Aaron Norman and illustrations by Michele Earle-Bridges.
　　　　p.　　cm.
　　Includes bibliographical references.
　　ISBN 0-8120-4669-2
　　1. Discus (Fish)　I. Vriends, Matthew M., 1937– .
　　II. Title.
SF458.D5G56　　1991
639.3'758 — dc20　　　　　　　　　　　91-13946
　　　　　　　　　　　　　　　　　　　　　　CIP

PRINTED IN HONG KONG

1234　　4900　　987654321

About the author:
Tom Giovanetti has been an aquarium hobbyist for many years. His articles have been published in most English-language aquarium magazines, and have been abstracted in other languages. At present, he is in charge of Research and Communication at Oceanic Systems, Inc., a manufacturer of aquariums and related equipment.

Photo credits: Aaron Norman: front cover; inside front cover; page 27 bottom; page 28; page 45 top, bottom right; page 46; page 63 top; inside back cover; back cover top, bottom right.
David Schleser: pages 9, 10, 11, 12; page 64 top.
Edward Taylor: page 27 top; page 45 bottom left; page 63 bottom, back cover bottom left.

Contents

Preface

Of the many fishes available for home aquariums, none has captured the fancy of aquarists quite like the discus. Though no other fish group, not even the colorful marines, inspires such apprehension and dedication in the fishkeeping soul, discus are not as difficult as their reputation (and many of their keepers) might lead you to believe.

Success in keeping discus is promoted by studying the animal's natural habitat. Where is the fish found? What is the chemistry of the water? What climatic cycles occur there? What makes up the bulk of the fishes' diet? We next must discover tolerable environmental parameters and attempt to approximate those conditions in our home aquariums. Though discus have been kept successfully for decades, technology today helps us to more easily simulate (**not** duplicate) the natural habitat of the discus. In fact, we can simulate it so closely that the discus will spawn and raise their young with little human intervention.

People keep discus for a variety of reasons. For some, the color, shape, and regal bearing of discus are an immediate attraction. Who would not be entranced by the metallic gleam of a large turquoise or cobalt discus under proper light? Most discus keepers start the hobby after seeing pictures of beautifully colored discus in tropical fish magazines or books. To a hobbyist who has become bored with traditional choices, the first glimpse of a colorful discus opens a new world.

Consider carefully whether discus are for you. Because they are more demanding of water quality than many other aquarium fish, discus require more water testing, more regular water changes, and more reliable filtration equipment than other fish do. A larger aquarium is necessary, at least 18 inches (45.5 cm) tall, and preferably no smaller than 30 gallons (113.4 L). Discus are not active, boisterous fish. They tend to hover quietly behind and under the leaves of plants, and move about in a regal, dignified manner. They do not frantically race around the aquarium, nor do they like companions that do. Their majestic bearing is one of the features that makes discus so attractive.

For some, discus keeping represents the highest level of the aquarium art, mainly because discus are among the most expensive aquarium fishes. This is because of the relative rarity of excellent specimens and the difficulties associated with breeding discus. One can often find small, generic discus at relatively moderate prices, but even these poor specimens are more expensive than most other fish in the retailer's tanks. High-quality discus, spawned and raised by one of but a handful of select breeders, are harder to find and are therefore more expensive.

Discus keeping also represents a pinnacle for the freshwater aquarist because of their reputed difficulty. Care problems have been exaggerated to the point that many hobbyists never attempt to keep discus, and many retail stores avoid carrying discus for the same reason. While discus are demanding fish, anyone willing to study and meet their needs will be rewarded with success.

Why keep discus? Because they are among the most beautiful and interesting aquarium fishes, as you will see.

The author and the editors of Barron's Series of Nature Books wish you much enjoyment with your discus. The author would also like to thank all those who had a part in the production of this book, including Dr. Matthew Vriends, Heiko Bleher, Dr. Paul Loiselle, Aaron Norman, but particularly Dr. David Schleser of the Dallas Aquarium, without whose expertise this volume would not have been possible.

Tom Giovanetti
Summer, 1991

Understanding Discus

Classification and Popular Names of Naturally Occurring Forms

Discus were discovered in 1840 by the Viennese ichthyologist, Dr. Johann Jacob Heckel. The earliest living specimens were shipped to Germany by airship in halves of 55-gallon (208 L) drums, and there were very heavy losses. It was not until the 1930s and 1940s that aquarium-fish dealers began importing discus into Europe and the United States under the common name "pompadour fish."

Discus are cichlids, which often surprises many aquarists. Discus, angelfish *(Pterophyllum sp.)*, and festivums *(Mesonauta festivus)* are all cichlids that occur together, though they possess features and exhibit behaviors that we do not usually associate with cichlids. Discus are the most extremely laterally compressed of all the cichlids, and they are peaceful, highly social fish that little resemble their cichlid relatives. Because they are not aggressive, they must not be kept with tankmates that will pick on them, chase them, and nip on their fins. Discus are not predatory, so they may be kept with even tiny fish without danger.

We will make a careful distinction between naturally occurring discus and tank-bred variants. Naturally occurring discus, though subject to limited variability, will usually have a pattern and color consistent with other specimens from the same area. Tank-bred variants, however, may be widely divergent from the original wild stock. Most fish available in the trade today are tank-bred variants.

Under the present classification, there are two species of discus, but four types, as one of the species contains three subspecies. Whether these are legitimate subspecies or simply ecophenotypes (geographical varieties) is a subject of disagreement. It is possible that all discus will be classified as the same species in the near future, but the

An ecophenotype is a group of organisms that share observable similarities in appearance that are distinguishable from others of the same species. These differences are based on isolation from the other members of the species and not on differences in physical structures.

classification scheme we use in this book is as follows:

1. *Symphysodon discus*, or the Heckel discus
2. *Symphysodon aequifasciata* sp., which consists of:
   a. *Symphysodon aequifasciata aequifasciata*, or the green discus
   b. *Symphysodon aequifasciata haraldi*, or the blue discus
   c. *Symphysodon aequifasciata axelrodi*, or the brown discus

The first species is *Symphysodon discus*, or the Heckel discus, sometimes called the blue Heckel or red Heckel, and rarely still called the pompadour discus. Heckel discus are native to the Manaus (Rio Negro) area in central Brazil. Of their nine vertical stripes, the first, fifth, and ninth stripes are pronounced, with the fifth noticeably thicker than the others. The first stripe runs through the eye, the fifth through the center of the body, and the ninth through the base of the tail. This thick center stripe is always present in Heckel discus. The fish has a mahogany background color, with faint blue stripes running horizontally through the body and with fins edged in red.

Heckel discus are the least marketable type, evidently because most hobbyists today prefer the turquoise striations more present on other types of discus, and because Heckel discus are more difficult to breed than other discus. Males breed somewhat more easily than females, so Heckel males are often crossbred with females of other species for the sake of their color and pattern, especially in Asia. The dark vertical stripes have proved very difficult to breed out of the line. Typically, aquarists want color, not black stripes, so the tank-bred Heckel discus are decreasing. This is unfortunate, as there should be hobbyists who seek to preserve the naturally occurring forms. Because of the relative lack of interest in cultivating the pure Heckel strain, almost all Heckel discus available today are caught wild. Heckel discus come from slightly warmer water than do other discus, and this should be taken into account when keeping them.

Symphysodon aequifasciata aequifasciata, or the green discus, is the nominate subspecies of the second species group. Most green discus come from the Putumayo River on the northern border of Peru and are shipped out of either Leticia, Colombia, or Iquitos, Peru. Many Peruvian green discus shipped out of Iquitos are captured in the Rio Nanay, which flows into the Amazon at Iquitos. Green discus are highly variable in pattern and color. The normal green discus has a background color that varies from brown to greenish-olive, with metallic horizontal stripes in the dorsal area and on the belly; these stripes extend into the dorsal and anal fins. The major portion of the body lacks these horizontal stripes, but red specks often are present on the sides. Green discus usually have more stripes than do brown discus. Strains of green discus having green stripes all over the body are often called royal green discus, which are in great demand.

Another variant of the green discus that is also popular, but very rarely available, is the Tefé discus, named after the Brazilian town and lake of Tefé on the Solimões. Some believe that the Tefé discus is a natural intergrade between the brown discus (*Symphysodon aequifaciata axelrodi*) and the green discus. Tefé discus have a greenish/gold background, with many red spots all over the midsection and the anal fin. Occasionally the red spots occur over the entire body, but always the first and last vertical stripes are thickened.

Parts of a discus.
1. Mouth.
2. Nostril.
3. Interorbital space.
4. Eye (orbit).
5. Nape (forehead).
6. Head.
7. Body.
8. Spinous dorsal fin.
9. Dorsal ridge.
10. Soft dorsal fin.
11. Caudal peduncle.
12. Caudal spines.
13. Tail (caudal fin).
14. Anal fin.
15. Pelvic fin.
16. Total length.
17. Standard length.
18. Pectoral fin.
19. Throat.
20. Operculum (gill cover).
21. Preopercle bone (cheek).

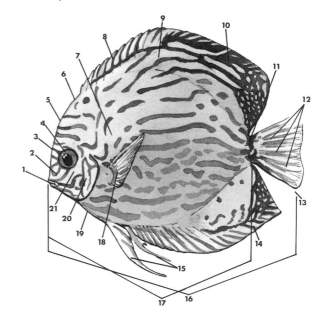

Understanding Discus

The turquoise discus is the dominant strain on the market today. In the turquoise strain, the natural greenish stripes of the green discus have been infused with a bluish color (possibly due to *S. a. haraldi* influence), resulting in horizontal stripes that vary from bluish-green to greenish-blue! Some turquoise discus are almost entirely blue on the body, and these are often called cobalt turquoise discus. Within the turquoise strain there are dozens of separate strains, with names like "brilliant turquoise," "red turquoise," and the like. The abundance of color strains can be bewildering to the beginner. Turquoise discus are more expensive than browns, greens, or Heckels, but are usually much more attractively colored.

The subspecies *Symphysodon aequifasciata axelrodi*, or the brown discus, comes from Belem near the mouth of the Amazon. The brown discus was once the most commonly kept discus in home aquariums, but it has recently been supplanted by the more colorful varieties. Brown discus range in color from light to dark brown and do not have the thickened fifth vertical band as does the Heckel discus. Striations on the brown discus appear on the forehead and anterior dorsium, and through the dorsal and anal fins. Some reddish specimens are occasionally found. Many of these reddish fish, unfortunately, do not owe their attractive coloration to genetics, but to food or chemicals in their culture water. Most so-called "red" discus bred in the Far East have had their colors brightened by being fed the eggs of the prawn *Macrobrachium rosenbergi* whose eggs contain abundant carotenes. The color returns to its normal brown only a few weeks after the fish have been weaned from this diet. Discus that have been thus unnaturally colored can usually be identified by the orange coloring of the muscular bases of their pectoral fins, the soft tissues around the eye, and the lip and snout area.

The third subspecies of *Symphysodon aequifasciata* is *Symphysodon aequifasciata haraldi*, the blue discus, from around Manaus. Blue discus strongly resemble their cousins, the brown discus, and for this reason some feel that blue discus are nothing more than nicely-colored brown discus. Unlike the brown discus, however, blue discus have a darker, almost purple-brown ground color, especially on the face. Blue horizontal stripes run across the head and dorsal and ventral areas. Blue discus with bright horizontal stripes throughout their bodies are called "royal blue discus," and the name is apt for really fine specimens. Too often, however, the name royal blue discus means little, for many blue discus are sold as royal blue because of the higher price they command. True royal blue discus are as fine a sight as you are likely to see in freshwater aquariums. There is another popular domestic strain of blue discus called cobalt blue or powder-blue discus. Cobalt blue discus are entirely blue or almost so, with little or no striation of any type. Cobalt blue discus have a metallic sheen that is quite attractive. They do not exist in nature, however, and therefore should not be confused with the wild blue discus.

These are the basic discus types that the hobbyist is most likely to encounter. As mentioned earlier, you will see many other strains, as well as unusual names like ghost discus, blue-faced discus, albino discus, and others. Until you develop some expertise at breeding discus, you would do best to stick with the mainstream types.

Are Discus Really Hard to Keep?

We spoke earlier of the reputation discus have for being hard to keep; we pointed out that this is not necessarily true. Discus are not so hard to maintain that you should be dissuaded from keeping them, but you cannot expect to be successful with discus by simply tossing a few of them into a typical community aquarium. This is so for several reasons:

Disease Sensitivity

Discus are more susceptible to common aquarium pathogens than many typical community aquarium fish are. It is particularly tricky to keep discus with angelfish and corydoras catfish, though some beginning discus keepers think that they can do just that. Almost all angelfish in the aquarium hobby are bred in captivity and frequently carry internal parasitic diseases to which discus seem especially prone. Because of the discus' demonstrable sensitivity to parasites and disease to which other aquarium fish are more resistant, it is obvious that the easiest way to keep your discus healthy is to keep them in a species tank (an aquarium in which a single species of fish is kept). It is possible, however, to keep discus mixed with angelfish (*Pterophyllum* sp.), provided you are sure that the angelfish are not carrying any disease organisms. Procedures for disinfecting such fish through quarantine and medication are discussed in the chapter, "Disease Recognition and Treatment."

Several other species of tropical fish make suitable tankmates for discus. A school of tetras (cardinal, neon, rummy nose, glowlight, emperor, Congo) makes an attractive display with discus, particularly if you resist the temptation to buy three or four of each, and instead keep a school of fifteen or twenty of a single species. I am particularly partial to combining a school of emperor tetras or the African Congo tetras with discus, though some purists may prefer the uniformity of keeping only South American species together. A pair of dwarf cichlids (*Papiliochromis ramirezi*) also does well, as do Clown Loaches (*Botia macracantha*), though all of these fish should be quarantined before being added to the discus aquarium. All these fish are very tolerant of the required water temperatures and conditions for discus. The chapter on the planted aquarium commends a few other suitable fish that are useful for algae control in a discus tank.

If you choose to keep your discus in a community aquarium, however, it's wise to regard the aquarium primarily as a discus tank with a few other species mixed in, and not vice versa. Keeping your priorities clearly in mind will help you make proper decisions when difficulties such as disease and parasite infestations occur.

Water Temperature Requirements

Discus require higher water temperatures than most other tropical aquarium fish. This is obvious from what has been reported about the natural habitat of discus. If discus are kept at temperatures suitable for most community aquarium fish—78°F (25.5°C)—they display a marked increase in disease susceptibility. For this reason, discus should be maintained between 82°F – 88°F (28°C – 31°C).

A question may arise here: don't other fish that share the discus' natural habitat seem perfectly at home at aquarium temperatures of between 77°F (25°C) and 79°F (26°C)? This is absolutely true, though many of these fish will not spawn unless the temperatures are elevated to normal habitat temperatures. These other fishes have demonstrated that their disease resistance and physiological tolerance extends down to 76°F (24.5°C), while the discus become significantly more susceptible to disease at temperatures lower than 82°F (27°C).

Timid Nature

Discus are somewhat shy fish that do not thrive in an aquarium with lots of active, boisterous fish or where there is bright, glaring light from which the discus have no retreat. You should not put discus in an aquarium with silver dollars, danios, or other highly active fish. It's also inadvisable to stock a discus aquarium too heavily with other species, as the stress that usually results from so varied a

Above: Two discus collectors string a net around a downed ▶ tree, a typical discus habitat.
Below: A third man climbs up the tree and shakes the branches in an attempt to drive the fish into the net. When these photos were taken in August 1988, discus collectors would receive approximately 50 cents for an adult discus!

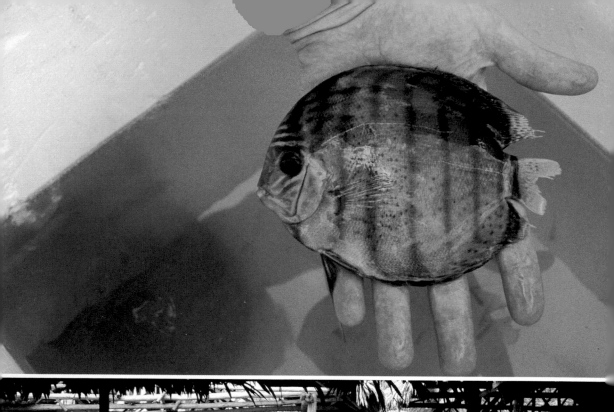

mixture of fish may be harmful to discus. Discus are quite sensitive to undue vibration, and other disturbances, moreover, so don't locate their aquarium in a high traffic area, such as a hallway.

Need for Good Water Quality

Most freshwater tropical fish are so tolerant of poor water quality that even careless aquarists are often successful. Discus, however, demand water of very high quality, so if you do not regularly monitor your water and make whatever adjustments are necessary, you are not likely to be very successful with discus.

It becomes clear, then, that discus are "more difficult" than other freshwater tropical fish only if you do not provide for them properly. As we have seen, their requirements are somewhat different from those of other freshwater tropicals. If you give your discus the attention they need, you will find them to be hardy, delightful, and long-lived.

The Amazon Habitat

Discus are native to the backwaters of the Amazon River and its tributaries in Brazil, Peru, Venezuela, and Colombia. These South American countries encompass the immense Amazon rain forest, generically called Amazonia. Discus are never found in the main body of the Amazon River, because the water is much too swift and silt laden. They are found in creeks (*igarapes*), feeder streams, and isolated pools, along with angelfish, festivums, severums, Uaru cichlids, and assorted characins.

Above: A freshly collected Peruvian green discus from Iquitos. Notice the characteristic red spots.
Below: A typical export operation in Iquitos. Notice the lack of a supplemental air supply. The water in the holding boxes is changed once or twice daily.

The tributary rivers have been classified into three types: the blackwater, white-water, and clear-water rivers. Blackwater rivers, or *agua preta*, are stained with humic acid from rotting organic matter from the jungle floor. Dead leaves and humus wash into the streams and rivers, where their decay produces carbon dioxide and humic acid. As a result, the so-called blackwater rivers are the color of tea or coffee. Despite this dark color, the water is not turbid, but fairly transparent, with a visibility of up to 5 feet (1.6 m). Blackwater contains few dissolved carbonate compounds and other minerals. This renders the water nearly devoid of buffering capacity, so the pH is easily influenced by humic acids. Mineral-free origin water, mingled with runoff water acidified by dissolved organics, causes the conductivity of blackwater to be very low, as low as 10 µs. (*microseimens*, see page 23). The pH of blackwater streams is also correspondingly low, often between 4 and 5.5 (see page 26). It is from blackwater, such as the Rio Negro (and areas where blackwater mixes with white water) that discus usually come.

The clear-water streams are green in color, with very high visibility, up to 15 feet (4.5 m). These waters have a higher pH than blackwater, although still acidic, with a pH between 5 and 6. Clear-water conductivity is also very low, around 15 µs. Though the pH of clear-water streams is acceptable to discus, they are not usually found in these streams. The current in clear-water rivers tends to be too swift for them, though discus are found in certain slower clear-water rivers. Well-known clear-water rivers include the Rio Xingu and the Rio Tapajos.

White water has a pH of between 6.4 and 7, conductivity of 25–60 µs., and an almost immeasurable total hardness (less than 1°dH, see page 22). Because it is rich in silt and sediment, however, white water is very turbid, with very little visibility. The water is not really "white," but looks yellow-beige. White water results from a mixture of the black and clear waters, with seepage of muddy nutrient springs. Typical white-water rivers are the Rio Solimões, Rio Madeira, and the Rio Branco.

Seasonal Changes

The seasonal flooding and ebbing of the Amazon and its tributaries is an important feature of life in Amazonia. The entire economy of the area revolves around it. About December the rainy season begins, and by late January the river and its myriad tributaries have swollen to huge proportions. It is during the rainy season that most Amazonian fish spawn. The Brazilian Amazon stays at flood level until June, and does not fall back to its lowest levels until just before the rains start again in December. In the upper or Peruvian Amazon, water levels are at their lowest during August and September. During the high water season, discus expand their range into the floodplain. As the flood begins to recede, temporary streams and residual lakes [*cochas*] are formed, draining back to the main river course. Many small landlocked ponds are also formed by this recession, and these become breeding pools for discus. Many of these pools are devoid of tree shade, so the water is warmed by the sun. This elevated temperature, often higher than 90°F (32.2°C), stimulates discus to spawn. Minor stagnation in the pools encourages blooms of microalgae and infusoria, and this microfauna provides an abundant source of food for young fish.

Some of the ponds where discus are found are located in heavily shaded areas. Since they receive little sunlight, these waters are significantly cooler, and these discus have been observed to be in poorer health and to have less reproductive success than those in warmer pools.

In a typical discus habitat, discus (along with festivums, severums, and angelfish) usually frequent protective undercut or vertical banks on the outer curves of rivers, or especially areas near banks where trees have fallen. Areas along the bank where a tree's elaborate root structure protrudes into the water are also frequented by discus. These structures provide the discus with protection, and are also areas where insects and other small food sources are likely to fall into the water. With their laterally compressed bodies, the discus easily glide between the branches and roots, and their vertical stripes and horizontal wavy stripes help to camouflage them.

Discus are often caught at night. The collectors spread their nets in an arc around a suitable section of bank, and then shine flashlights on the discus, temporarily blinding them. The fish are then scooped up with large hand nets or driven into the surrounding net, where they are gathered up and sorted according to size and color. A daytime technique is to surround a submerged tree with a net, and then have a collector climb out on the tree and jump up and down, frightening the discus into the net.

The discus spend between two to three weeks in the possession of collectors, exporters, and wholesalers before they are shipped to your local dealer. During this time they have been exposed to fluctuations in water purity, temperature, pH, and hardness, so it is easy to understand why they might not be in the greatest condition when, via importer and/ or wholesaler, they get to your local pet store. All fish outlets must carefully acclimate and care for the fish when they first arrive to ensure healthy, salable fish. The purchase of tank-bred discus may be preferable for the average discus keeper, because these fish have not undergone such trauma.

Water Chemistry and Filtration

The Importance of Filtration

The moment any living thing enters an aquarium it begins to change the water chemistry. Via their gills, fish take up oxygen dissolved in the water. As a result of this process, carbon dioxide (CO_2) is produced, which is released into the surrounding water (a physiological process called respiration). Fish also eat food and produce waste. All these processes chemically alter the water. In nature, such changes are compensated for by other processes to maintain stability. Because our aquariums are only approximations of nature, however, many of these balancing processes are absent. We

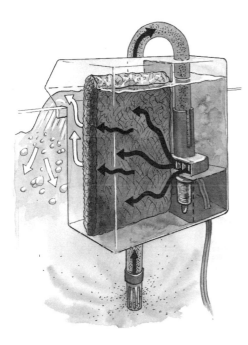

One of many box filter designs which hang on the back of the aquarium. Water from the aquarium is drawn up by suction from the pump impeller, which also forces the water through filter media before returning it to the aquarium.

must therefore intervene and compensate for chemical changes in the water with filtration. We cannot expect fish to do well if we require them to live in their own waste.

Historically, discus keepers have relied on large and frequent partial water changes to keep water quality high. As we will demonstrate, adequate filtration equipment plus regular small water changes is sufficient to provide the high water quality discus require.

All aquarium specimens require some degree of filtration to ensure good water quality, though some species demand better water quality than others. Experience has shown discus to be among the most demanding of aquarium water quality.

The three general types of aquarium filtration are biological, chemical, and mechanical. Each is critical to the maintenance of good water quality. We will discuss the processes that take place in nature, and we will then discuss the filtration equipment best suited to approximate natural conditions. Throughout this discussion, please bear in mind the important distinction between types of *filtration* and types of filtration *equipment*. Often one type of equipment can be made to perform more than one type of filtration.

The Nitrogen Cycle

All animals produce nitrogen as a component of their metabolic wastes. The form of nitrogen excreted depends on the habitat and physiology of the animal. Humans, for example, excrete urea, a concentrated form of nitrogen. We concentrate our nitrogen wastes because we cannot afford the fluid loss associated with excreting pure ammonia (NH_3). If humans excreted pure ammonia, we would dehydrate very quickly. Some desert animals, because they can afford almost no fluid loss, excrete solid crystals of urea. Fish, on the other hand, can afford great fluid loss, since they live totally immersed in water. They therefore excrete ammonia as a soluble gas.

Water Chemistry and Filtration

In nature, the nitrogen cycle converts organic animal wastes (ammonia and other nitrogen compounds) into beneficial plant fertilizer (nitrate). A brief explanation might be helpful.

Nitrification refers to the degradation of harmful nitrogen compounds by nitrifying bacteria. When inorganic ammonia (NH_3) is present, bacteria (*Nitrosomonas* sp.) convert the ammonia to nitrite (NO_2^-). In the discus aquarium, nitrite is more toxic than ammonia. Fortunately, other bacteria (*Nitrobacter* sp.) consume the nitrite and convert it to nitrate (NO_3^-), a relatively harmless compound that is the highest oxidized form of nitrogen. As a result, harmful wastes are converted into nitrates that benefit plants.

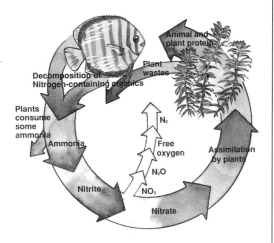

The Nitrogen Cycle. Wastes produced in the aquarium consist primarily of ammonia and other organic compounds. The organics break down into ammonia, which is reduced by nitrifying bacteria into nitrite. Some nitrogen blows out of solution as a gas, but most is further reduced by bacteria to nitrate. Some of the nitrate is consumed by plants as food, but most accumulates in the aquarium and must be diluted by regular partial water changes.

> The toxicity of ammonia is directly related to the pH of the water. At pH levels below neutral (7), ammonia occurs in a relatively harmless form (NH_4^+) called ammonium. At a pH above 7, however, ammonia (NH_3) is highly toxic.

Nitrifying bacteria grow on all surfaces in the aquarium. These bacteria must adhere to some surface in order to do their job. They also require oxygen in order to convert ammonia and nitrite. In fact, the more oxygen available to these bacteria, the faster they perform. The trick, then, is to provide a well-oxygenated surface to which the bacteria can adhere. After the bacteria have had time to reproduce sufficiently, all nitrogen wastes produced by fish in your aquarium will be reduced to nitrate before they reach measurable levels.

Nitrate levels above 20 mg/L (milligrams per liter) will stress the fish. Certain plants assimilate nitrate and other minerals (especially phosphate) rapidly enough to be considered a legitimate means of reducing nitrate, but most of the nitrate in an aquarium must be removed by regular partial water changes.

Biological Filtration

The most important type of aquarium filtration is biological filtration. The term "biological filtration" refers to the means by which aquarists harness and manage the nitrogen cycle in their aquariums.

Undergravel Filters: The most common type of biological filter is called an undergravel filter. An undergravel filter, usually made of injected plastic and perforated with numerous slots or holes, provides a false bottom for an aquarium. Two to three inches (5 – 7.7 cm) of gravel substrate is placed on top of the filter, completely burying the undergravel filter plate. Water is drawn up from under the undergravel filter via a lift tube, which displaces the water below the plastic plate. Water in the aquarium then seeps down through the gravel to

Water Chemistry and Filtration

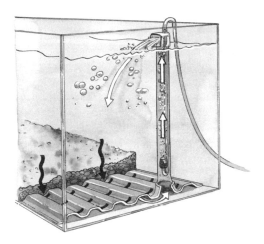

An undergravel filter. Water continually circulates through the substrate because of the displacement in the uplift tube by air bubbles produced by an airpump.

fill the void left by the water from under the filter plate. Nitrifying bacteria colonize the substrate because of the abundant surface area of the gravel on which the bacteria can attach themselves, and because the undergravel filter continually circulates oxygenated water and food (nitrogen compounds dissolved in the water) through the gravel. The engine that drives an undergravel filter is usually either an air pump or a submersible water pump called a power head. An undergravel filter circulates water in the aquarium, provides excellent biological filtration, and is at the same time inexpensive and unobtrusive. For many aquarists an undergravel filter is the best choice.

A disadvantage of undergravel filters is that they trap dirt and debris. This necessitates regular cleaning of the substrate, because the debris, if allowed to accumulate, will block the filter, decompose, and pollute the aquarium. You must be careful, however, not to overclean the substrate, remembering that the substrate harbors a culture of beneficial bacteria that maintain water quality. Disturbing the

nitrifying bacteria in the undergravel filter can result in a rise in ammonia and nitrite, which can lead to stress-induced disease or death for your fish. Another disadvantage of undergravel filtration is that if there should be a power outage lasting more than an hour or two, the effects can ruin the aquarium. If water stops circulating through the gravel, the bacteria in the substrate begin to die and decompose from lack of oxygen, and this pollutes the water.

For a discus aquarium with few or no live plants, an undergravel filter is an excellent biological filter, as long as it is faithfully maintained. Never clean the entire gravel substrate at one time. Clean only one third, or the top half inch, of the substrate each month. A commonly used tool for this job is a gravel vacuum, which consists of a piece of plastic siphon tubing with an open cylinder on one end. A gravel vacuum allows you to pick up the gravel in the cylinder, where the gravel swirls around and releases its debris. The dirty water is then siphoned out of the aquarium into a bucket. In this way the gravel may be cleaned in conjunction with a regular partial water change.

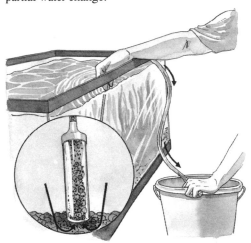

Vacuuming the substrate. Notice how the substrate swirls around in the vacuum, releasing debris that is siphoned off with the waste water.

Water Chemistry and Filtration

Canister Filters: A canister filter is a pressurized vessel containing various types of filter media. Water is drawn out of the aquarium, forced through the media, and then pumped back up to the aquarium. Because it operates outside (and usually below) the aquarium, it can be as large as necessary and is therefore very efficient. Because canister filters are pressurized, it is possible to make maximum use of the filtration medium by forcing the water through it.

Canister filters are often used in conjunction with undergravel filters, and as such are used primarily as mechanical and chemical filters. In situations where undergravel filters are not used, a canister filter can be used as a dedicated biological filter. If we want to use a canister filter for biological filtration, we need a medium that has a lot of surface area on which the bacteria can colonize, but yet will not clog or trap dirt. Several such media are available, including small ceramic tubes (often called "noodles"), and inert plastic devices called "bioballs" or "biospheres." Both of these are ideal as biological media in a canister filter, as they have high surface area and will not trap dirt. If you choose a canister filter for biological filtration, remember several things: First, *never turn the filter off for more than a half hour*, as the bacteria in the filter will die if their oxygen supply is cut off, and their remains will pollute the aquarium with hydrogen sulfide when the filter is turned back on. When cleaning or servicing the canister filter, remember that critical bacteria are colonized on the medium, and *don't clean, rinse, or otherwise disturb the biological medium*. Also, *remember to use no more than one inch (2.5 cm) of gravel substrate in the aquarium if your are not using an undergravel filter*. If you do not use an undergravel filter, water does not circulate through the substrate, so if the substrate is too deep, debris such as uneaten food particles and solid wastes will settle down into the gravel and decompose, releasing harmful byproducts such as hydrogen sulfide. Hydrogen sulfide is that "rotten egg" odor you smell in hoses or filters where

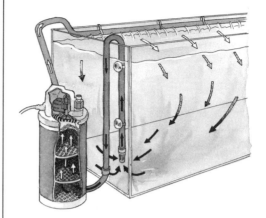

A canister filter. Unlike box or trickle filters, the canister filter is pressurized, so it may be placed almost anywhere—either beneath or beside the aquarium. Water is drawn into the canister by suction from a built-in impeller pump and is forced through various types of filtration media before being returned (here via a spray bar) to the aquarium.

water has stagnated. When stagnation occurs in an aquarium substrate, anaerobic bacteria take over, the gravel turns black, and small bubbles rise up. Regular maintenance of the gravel substrate will prevent the "packing" of the substrate that leads to hydrogen sulfide production.

Trickle Filters: Trickle filters (sometimes called wet/dry filters) are extremely efficient devices for biological filtration. Remember, nitrifying bacteria work best when given lots of oxygen. In an undergravel filter, or indeed any submerged media, the amount of oxygen available to the nitrifying bacteria is limited to the oxygen-holding capacity of the water. Another drawback of submerged biological media is that the nitrifying bacteria are competing with the fish for dissolved oxygen. Both bacteria and fish are extracting dissolved oxygen from the same water, so neither have as much oxygen available as they might otherwise.

Water Chemistry and Filtration

Trickle filters use a filter medium with lots of surface area (like the plastic spheres mentioned earlier), but the medium is supported out of the water, exposed to the air. Water from the aquarium is constantly trickled over the medium, so it stays damp at all times. Only a thin layer of aquarium water covers the medium, so the bacteria on the filter medium have access to an unlimited supply of oxygen from the air. And the bacteria are not taking dissolved oxygen away from the fish; in fact, the drops of water trickling over the filter medium are actually supersaturated with oxygen as they fall through the trickle filter.

It may seem at this point that a trickle filter is the ideal biological filter for all aquariums, and this is largely true. For marine and most freshwater aquariums the trickle filter is ideal. It has one other characteristic, however, that must be considered:

trickle filters tend to raise the pH (alkalinity) of aquarium water by *degassing*.

The carbon buffering cycle in water is a very complex process whereby organic carbon (from plant and animal waste) is broken down by bacteria and/or assimilated by plants. A result of this process is the release of free carbon dioxide (CO_2) into the water, some of which forms carbonic acid. Much of this carbon dioxide passes out of the water and into the atmosphere, and some is consumed by plants, but some CO_2 also acts as a stabilizing agent in the bicarbonate/carbonate acid system. Basically, what this means to aquarists is that if there is not enough CO_2 in the water, the pH will rise, and if there is too much CO_2 in the water for the amount of carbonate and bicarbonate salts present, the pH may drastically fall to 4.5 or below.

Trickle filters, because of their degassing (very high gas exchange) ability, blow large amounts of CO_2 out of aquarium water. This is great in marine aquariums or freshwater African cichlid aquariums, since both of these aquariums need elevated pH levels, but for fish like discus, which prefer slightly acidic water, trickle filters would be detrimental to the pH without the use of chemical acidifiers, or the addition of supplemental CO_2 (see chapter, "The Planted Discus Aquarium," for more on CO_2 addition). There is no question that a trickle filter would be ideal for a discus aquarium, so long as the pH is maintained at acceptable levels.

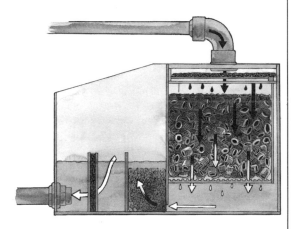

A trickle ("wet/dry") filter. Water from the aquarium is trickled over an inert media (here, ceramic "noodles"). Bacteria cultured on the media convert ammonia and nitrite into nitrate. The water may then be drawn through other filtration media before being pumped back up to the aquarium.

Good filtration equipment provides all the aeration that is necessary. In fact, excessive aeration is harmful to the discus aquarium, because the large, abundant air bubbles produced by aeration remove carbon dioxide (CO_2), thus raising the pH of the water. This loss of carbon dioxide would be especially harmful to live plants, which need abundant carbon dioxide as a primary nutrient.

Water Chemistry and Filtration

Natural System: A unique way to biologically filter a discus aquarium is to use the so-called "natural" system. Remembering that nitrifying bacteria colonize all surfaces in the aquarium, and taking into account that live plants consume ammonia and nitrite, a densely planted aquarium, appropriately stocked, can theoretically handle all the nitrogen wastes produced by the fish. Maintenance of such an aquarium is tricky, but possible, and is best left to experienced aquarists. Even one overfeeding can destabilize the aquarium. Interestingly enough, the natural system, which is often considered a recent innovation, is how freshwater aquariums were almost always kept in the earliest years of the hobby, when the old books referred to the "balanced aquarium." Mild additional aeration is often necessary in a natural system, especially at night. A variation on the natural system is described in the chapter, "The Planted Discus Aquarium."

Chemical Filtration

Biological filtration takes care of nitrogen, but not all fish waste is ammonia and nitrite. A significant portion is composed of chemicals such as phenols, dyes, and proteins, usually in a liquid or soluble form. If these and other dissolved organics are not removed by some form of filtration, they will build up to unacceptable levels and cause that familiar yellowish coloration so well known to aquarists. Further, if dissolved organics reach sufficient levels they can cause stress to fish by reducing dissolved oxygen levels, as well as by encouraging the growth of harmful bacteria. The removal of dissolved organics and other unwanted compounds from aquarium water is called **chemical filtration**.

Activated Carbon: The most common agent of chemical filtration is activated carbon (**not** ordinary charcoal). Dissolved organics are first absorbed and then adsorbed, but adsorption is by far the most significant process. Each individual grain of carbon has enormous surface area because of the numerous pores and crevices caused by activation. It is this tremendous amount of surface area that makes activated carbon so effective, because dissolved organic compounds become bound to these surfaces through adsorption.

Through regular use of activated carbon you can remove dyes (in urine), phenols, uric acid and other yellowing matter, growth limiting hormones emitted by both fish and plants, excess nutrients that cause algal growth (such as phosphate), dissolved organics that affect pH and dissolved oxygen levels, and products of the decomposition of uneaten food and fish wastes. Activated carbon also quickly removes medication from the water after treatment has concluded. Clearly, activated carbon is a resource few aquariums can do without.

Activated carbon is an indiscriminate adsorber: in other words, it removes both beneficial and harmful substances. Along with undesirable dissolved organic pollution, activated carbon also removes such things as vitamins, medications, and important plant nutrients (especially iron). Though activated carbon does remove some helpful compounds, it removes so many harmful chemicals that its use is strongly recommended, and we can supplement trace element depletion through regular partial water changes.

Usually activated carbon is placed in a fine mesh filter bag and used in some type of forced-flow filter, such as a canister or box filter. When choosing activated carbon, look for small granules rather than pellets. Granular carbon has far more surface area than pellets, so it will last considerably longer. Some grades of activated carbon are tiny slivers, and these have the greatest possible surface area. Some brands of carbon are available in their own filter bag, but you can usually also buy bulk carbon and reusable drawstring filter bags at a pet store.

Be sure to rinse the carbon before putting it in the filter, though better grades of carbon have very little carbon dust. Water should be forced through the carbon at a slow, steady rate. In a canister filter, for instance, the carbon bag should entirely fill the diameter of the canister in all directions, so that the water cannot easily flow around the carbon instead of through it. Also, position the carbon so that the water flows through it **after** the water has already been mechanically filtered, so the carbon does not get clogged with dirt and slime. In fact, when using filtration media in series, mechanical filtration should always precede chemical and biological filtration.

Molecular Adsorption Resins: Molecular adsorption resins are very useful for removing undesirable chemical elements from the aquarium water. They also remove some ammonia, nitrite, and nitrate, but not at sufficient rates to replace biological filtration. Another important use of molecular adsorption resins is removal of medications after their use has been discontinued.

Molecular adsorption resins are available in several forms. It is possible to buy them in a porous filter bag for use with a canister or trickle filter. As the resin is used up it darkens to a blackish color. When all the resin has become discolored, it must be either discarded or recharged, using the recharging process detailed for the particular product. The recharging feature is a major advantage over activated carbon, though the time span between recharges gets shorter and shorter, until eventually the resin must be replaced.

You can also get molecular adsorption resins in an impregnated fiber pad. Again, in pad form the resin is intended to be used in a canister filter or box filter. An advantage of a fiber resin pad is that it can be cut to fit whatever filter configuration you use.

There has been some disagreement among experts on the effectiveness of molecular adsorption resins as compared with activated carbon. Both are useful, and they are not redundant when used together. In fact, it is possible to buy an effective combination of activated carbon and molecular adsorption resin beads in a single filter bag. With such a mix, however, the resin cannot be recharged.

Ozone: Another effective method of chemical filtration is the use of ozone. Ozone is a very unstable form of oxygen; whereas a normal molecule of free oxygen (O_2) has two oxygen atoms, a molecule of ozone (O_3) has three oxygen atoms. This extra oxygen atom makes the ozone molecule very unstable, because the ozone molecule inclines toward yielding its extra oxygen atom to something and go back to being stable oxygen. It is this tendency to donate an oxygen atom that makes ozone a potent *oxidizer*, and thus a powerful agent of chemical filtration. When ozone comes in contact with dissolved organics, it oxidizes them, literally burning them up. Ozone is also helpful for killing bacteria and protozoans in water. Because of its powerful oxidizing capability, ozone is often used to purify bottled water for human consumption.

The problem with ozone is that it is such a powerful oxidizer that it can cause damage to a fish's sensitive membranes, such as gill and skin tissues. Despite its instability, ozone does stay in solution for a time, so it is imperative that free ozone not be allowed to enter the aquarium water or escape into an enclosed room. This means that ozone gas should be used only in some type of reaction chamber. In marine aquariums ozone is commonly used in a device known as a protein skimmer. Protein skimmers use very fine air bubbles to attract dissolved organic compounds and float them up a reaction chamber, where they are removed in a collection cup. Protein skimmers are mostly ineffective in fresh water, however, because fresh water is not dense enough to produce the fine air bubbles necessary for organics removal. Some discus keepers, however, use protein skimmers simply as reaction chambers for ozone. No other method of chemical filtration is as effective as ozone for clarifying the water and eliminating disease organisms.

If you use ozone, use it only in a separate reaction chamber, and be sure that the water exiting the reaction chamber passes through activated carbon before it reenters the aquarium. The activated carbon will adsorb any free ozone still present in the water and will remove those organic chemicals that have been oxidized but not removed by the ozone.

Water Chemistry and Filtration

Water Changes as Filtration: No matter how efficient your filtration equipment, your aquarium will need periodic partial water changes. After aquarium water has been depleted by fish and intense filtration certain trace elements have been exhausted, and others may have built up to stressful proportions. Regular partial water changes dilute any accumulation of compounds that have not been removed by your filtration equipment, and replace critical missing compounds. The amount of water and frequency of changes will vary from aquarium to aquarium, but in an aquarium incorporating sufficient biological, chemical, and mechanical filtration, changing 20–30 percent of the aquarium water each month is about right. This may strike some as too few water changes, because larger, more frequent water changes were once advocated for discus. With improvements in aquarium filtration, however, monthly water changes larger than 20–30 percent are not necessary. You may need to increase the number of water changes if you are attempting to breed your discus.

Overfiltration?: It is important to note that it is possible to overfilter aquarium water. Filter the water as efficiently as possible, and do regular partial water changes. This ensures that the aquarium water is clean and healthful, and replaces portions of the water before the entire volume of aquarium water has been stripped of its essential elements.

Mechanical Filtration

Mechanical filtration is the least important of the three types, but it is the one most people think about when they think of aquarium filtration, because the results are so obvious.

Mechanical filtration is the process intended to remove particulate matter from aquarium water. Aquariums constantly produce solid waste, because some food goes uneaten, some plant leaves fall off and break apart, and some fish waste remains in solid form. Mechanical filtration is used to remove this detritus because it is unsightly, and because it will eventually break down into dissolved organic pollution, discolor the aquarium water, and spoil the water quality.

Aquarists want their aquariums to be crystal clear, but fish do not care whether the water is clear or murky. In fact, discus come from waters that are often turbid and stained with organic dyes. Some slight water discoloration from humus should usually be present in a discus aquarium, especially in a breeding aquarium, but what aquarist wants to use a flashlight to see his fish? Thus, mechanical filtration is needed for the fishkeeper as well as for the fish.

The most common medium for mechanical filtration is floss. Synthetic floss is used to trap particulate waste. When the floss is sufficiently dirty, it is removed, along with the dirt it has absorbed. The more often you replace your filter medium, the cleaner your aquarium water will be. Most aquarists use either a canister or box filter for mechanical filtration. Box filters hang on a wall of the aquarium. A small pump draws water up, forces it through some filter medium, and then returns the water to the aquarium. Often box filters have compartments for both filter floss and activated carbon. Box filters are available in sizes for small to large aquariums, though box filters are commonly used for smaller aquariums of 20 gallons (75.6 L) or less. For larger aquariums a canister filter is a better option. A canister filter can incorporate filter floss for mechanical filtration, activated carbon and molecular adsorption resins for chemical filtration, and ceramic noodles for biological filtration. In such an arrangement, you might replace the filter floss weekly, the activated carbon monthly, the molecular adsorption resin bimonthly, and (of course) never change the ceramic noodles. Because canister filters are sealed, it is very easy to let regular maintenance slip. Don't wait until the water stops coming out of the filter to service it! Disconnect your canister filter and replace fouled media at least once a month.

Water Chemistry and Filtration

An old-fashioned immersed corner filter. This filter is filled with activated carbon and synthetic floss, and is then placed in the aquarium. Air injected into the filter from an air pump displaces water inside the filter, which allows water from the aquarium to be continually drawn into and through the filter.

A third type of mechanical filtration is submicronic filtration. This uses a filter that forces water through a very fine filter sleeve or pleat. As the name implies, submicronic filter pleats have a very fine mesh, with a pore size of around .2 microns. This tiny pore size is certainly smaller than any particle of dirt; in fact, it is smaller than many free-swimming parasitic organisms. Because the filter is so fine, it is necessary to prefilter the water with a rougher grade of mechanical filter before the water reaches the submicronic pleat. The flow rate of the water through the pleat is slow, often around 20 gallons (75.6 L) per hour.

Submicronic filtration pleats are usually housed in a canister that can be used in series with other filtration canisters. In one system, the first canister contains a floss filter, the second contains activated carbon, the third contains molecular adsorption

resins, and the fourth contains a submicronic filtration pleat. This system produces water of very high quality. Provided you have room below or near your discus aquarium, such a series of pressurized canisters is very highly recommended. When using such an efficient filtration system, remember the need for regular partial water changes to replace necessary trace elements.

As we discussed earlier, if you use undergravel filters it is important to keep them as free of dirt as possible. One way to dramatically cut down on the need for gravel cleanings is to use either a box or canister filter to constantly "vacuum" the aquarium water clear of dirt. Because most of the dirt gets trapped in the mechanical filter of either the box or canister, it never gets to the undergravel filter.

A diatom filter is a pressurized vessel in which water is forced through a paper pleat. A fine white powder composed of the skeletons of tiny organisms called diatoms is impregnated into the pleat. Diatom filters are capable of such fine filtration that it is often called "water polishing." Because of their fine, submicronic filtration, however, diatom filters clog easily (often within a matter of hours), so diatom filters are not intended for continuous duty. You may want to use a diatom filter for a few hours once every week or so, or you might use it only when the water gets cloudy or dingy. As with any canister filter, be sure to rinse and drain the filter and pleat whenever you store it for an extended period.

The Carbon Cycle

Many aquarists need not concern themselves with water hardness, but an understanding of water hardness and the other implications of the carbonate/bicarbonate cycle is critical for anyone who expects to keep discus successfully.

Water Hardness

Carbonate Hardness: As soon as rainwater reaches the ground it begins to be affected by the minerals in the soil through which it passes. Typically, rainwater percolates through topsoil and absorbs carbon dioxide from decaying plant matter and the respiration of plant roots. As a result the rainwater becomes slightly acidic, because the carbon dioxide (CO_2) reacts with the water (H_2O) to form carbonic acid (H_2CO_3). The carbonic acid, in turn, dissolves calcium carbonate ($CaCO_3$) [limestone] in sedimentary rock to form calcium bicarbonate [$CA(HCO_3)_2$]. The presence of calcium carbonate and bicarbonate in water produces carbonate hardness, which is measured in German degrees of Carbonate Hardness (°dCH).

Noncarbonate Hardness: As the water continues to move through the soil and rock, it picks up many other mineral elements, especially sulphates, chlorides, nitrates, magnesium, barium, and strontium. The amount of hardness caused by the accumulation of these elements is called noncarbonate hardness which is usually measured in German degrees of Noncarbonate Hardness (°dNCH).

General Hardness: General hardness (°dH) is total hardness—the sum of carbonate and noncarbonate hardness. Another scale that is commonly used is milligrams per liter of calcium carbonate (mgL $CaCO_3$).

°dH	mg/L $CaCO_3$	Considered
3	0–50	Soft
3–6	50–100	Moderately Soft
6–12	100–200	Slightly Hard
12–18	200–300	Moderately Hard
18–25	300–450	Hard
Over 25	Over 450	Very Hard

[1 mg/L = 1 part per million (ppm)
1°dH = 17.9 ppm]

Carbonate hardness can be reduced by boiling the water, because boiling causes the bicarbonates to break apart and precipitate (turn to solid form). For this reason carbonate hardness is often called "temporary hardness," to contrast it with noncarbonate hardness, or "permanent hardness."

Human beings take water hardness for granted, noting only that soap lathers better in soft water. For fish, however, water hardness is critical, because the mineral content in the water affects the osmotic pressure with which the fish and (especially) their eggs must cope. It is important to keep fish in water that is similar to that from which they were taken, for if soft-water fish are put in very hard water, they will be under constant stress and their eggs may not be fertilized successfully. Water hardness also affects the regulation of the fish's blood calcium level, so significant differences between a fish's native water hardness and its aquarium environment require the fish to work harder to maintain its blood calcium level.

Though discus are not very tolerant of fluctuations in many water parameters, discus have proven to be remarkably adaptable to varying degrees of hardness in aquarium water, thriving in water with a general hardness of over 20°dH (358 ppm $CaCO_3$). It is only when breeding discus that having lower water hardness levels (around 3–4°dH) is important, because in harder water, the shells of the eggs become abnormally resistant to penetration by sperm. In general, discus will do very well in tap water, requiring softened water only when spawning, at which time the eggs only—not the fish—require softened water. In fact, the young discus are easily raised in hard water. You can go to great lengths to keep the hardness of your aquarium water very low, near that of the discus' native habitat, or you can adapt your discus to hardness levels more typical of *your* native habitat! Most tank-raised discus are raised in slightly hard water (between 9 and 12°dH). If you purchase such fish, they probably have already been acclimated to a certain degree to higher levels of water hardness. You will actually have fewer disease problems if you keep your discus in slightly hard water, because the higher salt content of slightly hard water discourages bacterial proliferation. In general, discus should not be kept in water that is harder than $18°dH$ [320 ppm $CaCO_3$], with around $11°dH$ [200 ppm $CaCO_3$] being a convenient ideal. Because the tap water in many areas is significantly higher than $18°dH$, some softening of the tap water will probably still be necessary for most aquarists.

Recommended Water Hardness for *Keeping Discus*: $10 - 15°dH$

Recommended Water Hardness for *Breeding Discus:* $3 - 10°dH$

Osmoregulation

Because the body fluids of fresh water fish contain more salt than their habitat waters, freshwater constantly seeps through the skin and gills of freshwater fish and dilutes their body fluids. For this reason, freshwater fish drink very little water and excrete large amounts of water. Marine fish, on the other hand, cannot afford as much fluid loss as freshwater fish, as they lose fluids through their skin and gills, and must constantly drink water (and separate out the salts) to avoid dehydration.

The osmotic balance between fish and water is therefore at least partially dependent on the consistency of the salt concentration in the surrounding water. Drastic changes in the salt content of aquarium water are capable of causing "osmotic shock" in sensitive aquarium fish. The quantity of dissolved salts in the water can be measured in terms of the water's conductivity. Because salt conducts a weak electrical current, a conductivity meter measures the electrical conductivity of the water, thus indirectly measuring the amount of dissolved salts in the water. Conductivity measurements are often said to measure water hardness, but this is not an accurate way to state results of conductivity measurement. It is accurate to say that the higher the conductivity, the harder the water, but conductivity measurements only generally indicate water hardness measurements.

Conductivity is measured in microseimens (μs.). Though the native waters of discus often show amazingly low conductivity measurements of 10–60 μs., levels this low are extremely difficult to maintain in aquarium water, so a conductivity level of between 300–675 μs. is the target for a discus aquarium. The low end of that range is appropriate for breeding discus, with the high end acceptable for maintaining discus.

Conductivity measurements are useful because they are extremely accurate. A conductivity meter, however, is rather expensive, so only the most serious discus keepers and breeders will find a conductivity meter useful. It is possible to purchase a meter which measures both conductivity and pH, depending on the probe used. Unfortunately, it is impossible to measure conductivity in any other way than with an electronic meter.

Controlling Water Hardness in Tap Water

Though the recommended general hardness of between 10–15°dH is significantly higher than the discus' natural habitat, it is still fairly low, and chances are you will have to soften your tap water somewhat to reach this level. Be sure to test the pH and general hardness of your tap water with an accurate test kit before making any alterations to the water hardness.

The most accurate way to measure pH and hardness is with an electronic meter. These meters are handy and accurate, but expensive, and require periodic calibration to maintain their accuracy. The many liquid and powdered reagent test kits available in aquarium shops are accurate enough for most hobbyists. Be sure to follow the manufacturer's instructions and note the shelf life of the reagents and the waiting time for the reagents to give accurate results. You should always test the pH and general hardness of tap water used for partial water changes and evaporation top-up before using, and adjust as necessary.

Filtering through Peat: One-time honored way to soften tap water is by filtering it through peat. Peat, which is slightly acidic, acts as a cation (positively charged ion) exchanger and replaces the calcium dissolved in the water (as calcium bicarbonate) with hydrogen ions: $(H_2/peat) + Ca(HCO_3)_2 = (Ca/peat) + 2CO_2 + H_2O$. The hydrocarbonate is thus transformed into carbon dioxide. Peat has a way of gently and gradually lowering the hardness of the water. Since it also adds humic acids that discus and other Amazonian fishes find so important, the use of peat to soften tap water is highly recommended. If used too long, however, peat decomposes, and releases all the minerals it has absorbed. For this reason you do not want to leave peat in a canister filter for too long. Peat is best used to soften tap water down to the desired level and then discarded. If the hardness of your water supply isn't too high, you may need only to dilute it with a quantity of peat-filtered water to achieve the desired hardness level.

Peat is available in a wide variety of grades. Black "sedge" peat is useless and dangerous, because it will quickly dissolve into muck. Peat from Germany or the north-central United States is quite suitable. It is best to purchase peat designed for softening aquarium water from an aquarium store.

There are some drawbacks to peat filtration. Peat slightly discolors the water, which somewhat reduces light penetration into the aquarium. This can be a problem in a planted aquarium if the available lighting is marginal. Too much discoloration may be objectionable from an aesthetic standpoint, but use of activated carbon will remove the stain from the peat without increasing the water hardness. Also, in the planted aquarium, peat seems to release substances into the water that can depress plant growth, but activated carbon will also solve this problem. Neither of these drawbacks should dissuade aquarists from using limited amounts of peat filtration to treat tap water when necessary.

It is possible to achieve many of the benefits of peat filtration without using peat. Several commercial preparations of "blackwater extract" are available that condition tap water to its soft, acidified state simply by adding the proper amount of extract. For keeping discus, addition of blackwater extract may be all that is necessary; further water softening is necessary for the successful hatching of discus eggs.

Dilution with Rainwater: Another method of softening tap water is to dilute it with rainwater, though this has become a problem in many places because rainwater often picks up chemical pollutants as it falls through the atmosphere. If rainwater is filtered through activated carbon, however, the chemical pollutants are removed and the rainwater is safe to use. Rainwater is naturally soft because it has not yet accumulated mineral salts from the ground.

The use of either peat or rainwater dilution is probably sufficient for those who want to keep discus in good health in their aquariums, but if you intend to breed discus, you will probably need more sophisticated water softening methods.

Ion Exchange Resins: Ion exchange resins fall into two categories, anion exchangers and cation exchangers. Anions are negatively charged ions, and cations are positively charged ions. Ion exchange resins are usually housed in a clear acrylic cylinder through which water is forced under pressure from a pump. The resins have a limited capacity, and must be either replaced or recharged when they have been exhausted.

Ordinary water-softening resins commonly sold for home and laundry use are unsuitable for aquarium use because they result in too many sodium ions. Therefore, if you use ion exchange resins, use only those sold for use to soften *aquarium* water. In a typical two-column aquarium ion exchange reactor, positively charged ions (cations) such as calcium and magnesium are replaced with hydrogen in the first column, and negatively charged ions (anions) such as bicarbonate and sulphate are replaced with hydroxyl ions in the second column. The resulting water is too soft, however, and must be diluted with tap water to restore necessary trace elements for the fish and essential nutrients for plants. This water must also be allowed to stand or aerated to force excess carbon dioxide out of the water.

It is better to use a partial cation deionizer, which exchanges positively charged ions such as calcium with hydrogen ions. This method eliminates only bicarbonate hardness while leaving most of the necessary trace elements behind, thus eliminating the need for dilution with tap water. While such a partial deionizer does depress the pH by producing an excess of carbon dioxide, this is no problem when preparing water for discus, and the excess carbon dioxide will eventually blow out of solution or be used up by plants.

It's always a good idea to discard the first gallon or so of water produced by ion exchange resins, because it is possible for the initial water to contain ammonia compounds which are toxic to fish.

Note that the primary purpose of ion exchange resins is the treatment of tap water. Ion exchange resins should not be continuously used on aquarium water, because they will remove too many important buffering elements from the water, resulting in a possible "acid fall" of the aquarium pH, and because water entirely stripped of trace elements is not healthy for either fish or plants.

Ion exchangers have several drawbacks. There are many different resins available, so there may be confusion over which resin is best for your application. More important: ion exchange resins have to be frequently recharged with highly concentrated acids or bases. Even under supervision of trained technicians these chemicals are dangerous, so the hobbyist should think twice before handling them. Even if recharged properly, ion exchange resins lose about 30 percent of their effectiveness each year, and they are very expensive to replace when

necessary. Also, while the effluent from the ion exchange process is indeed very soft, it is not pure. It still may contain dissolved organics, and even bacteria. For these reasons another method of softening tap water is probably a better choice for most discus keepers, and that method is reverse osmosis.

Reverse Osmosis Filtration: Reverse osmosis filters are the ultimate in tap water filtration. The principle of reverse osmosis has been used for kidney dialysis and desalinizing drinking water from seawater aboard ships, and RO water is very useful for the maintenance of rain forest plants such as orchids. RO filters, as they are called, are somewhat more expensive than ion exchangers to set up (though the initial cost has dropped dramatically in recent years), but they have significantly lower running costs and require much less maintenance. RO filters produce a purer product without the mess, bother, and complication of ion exchangers, and with RO units there is no risk of ammonia contamination. Maintenance of the RO unit does not entail the use of dangerous chemicals, and the final product is superior drinking water; in fact, many commercial water coolers in offices and homes use RO purification. Be aware, however, that since RO water has had its chlorine and chloramine removed, attention must be given to the way in which RO water is stored, because it has no protection against bacterial contamination. This is true, of course, of *any* dechlorinated water, including ion exchanged water.

Reverse osmosis filters are superior to ion exchangers in that they do not exchange anything; at no point in the process do they exchange "bad" substances for "less bad" substances. RO filters first filter out fine particles, chlorine, and chloramine from tap water with a disposable 1.5 micron filter, and then force the water across a spiral-wound semipermeable membrane at around 60 psi (pounds per square inch), which separates the source water into deionized and slightly more mineralized (10 to 25 percent harder than the source water) reject water. The reject water is bypassed through a separate tube, and can be used for watering plants and for African cichlid and livebearer aquariums, in which alkaline water is preferable. This process results in water that is 94 to 99 percent pure (depending on the membrane).

Two types of membrane are used on reverse osmosis systems: TFC (Thin Film Composite) and CTA (Cellulose Triacetate). Choice of membranes depends on your source water and on your needs. CTA membranes are very tolerant of chlorine in the source water; in fact, they require chlorine in the source water because they are very susceptible to bacterial attack on the cellulose fibers in the membrane. For this reason CTA membranes are not appropriate for those who use well water. CTA membranes cannot be used on source water with dissolved solids higher than 500 ppm, or on water that has a pH higher than 8.5. TFC membranes are able to handle water that is extremely hard (up to 3,000 ppm dissolved solids) such as seawater and water from private wells. TFC membranes are very resistant to bacteria, and they are particularly suited for rejecting nitrate, phosphate, and silicates. The single drawback of a TFC membrane is its intolerance of chlorine. Because almost all municipal water sources chlorinate the water, municipal water must first be run through an activated carbon filter before being passed over a TFC membrane.

Both membranes require water temperature under 85°F (29.4°C), so you should install your RO unit in such a way that it is impossible to accidentally run hot water through the RO unit. Freezing will also destroy the membrane, so the unit should be installed on an indoor line that never freezes. Membranes should never be allowed to dry out, so if you anticipate not using your unit for an extended period of time, remove the membrane and store it in the refrigerator in a plastic bag with some water.

RO units typically yield about 20 percent; in other words, they produce 1 gallon (3.7 L) of permeate (filtered water) and 4 gallons (14.8 L) of concentrate (mineralized water) for every 5 gallons (19 L) of water. The membranes must be flushed

regularly (after about 150 operational hours or once a week) and usually replaced in two to three years. Other than regular flushing and biennial replacement of the membrane, there is no maintenance, supplemental purchases, or recharging necessary. Because the initial cost of an RO unit has fallen dramatically within the last few years, RO units are now within reach of the average hobbyist.

Remember, deionized water has virtually no buffering capacity. Whichever method of water softening you use, you must dilute it with enough tap water to adjust the hardness and pH to the recommended levels. The only sure way to do this is to use a test kit or electronic gauge for water hardness and pH.

pH

The acidity or alkalinity of water is measured in units of pH, or power of hydrogen (*pondus hydrogenii*), on a scale from 0 to 14. A pH of 7 is neutral, with numbers lower than 7 acidic and numbers higher than 7 alkaline. The pH scale is a logarithmic scale, so a pH of 8 is ten times more alkaline than a pH of 7, and a pH of 9 is one hundred times more alkaline than a pH of 7. Obviously, a quick change in pH from 6.0 to 4.5 is a traumatic (and possibly fatal) change for a fish.

Many factors affect the pH of water, including the amount of dissolved carbon dioxide, but the hardness of the water is especially significant. For this reason water hardness is said to"buffer" pH. "Buffering" is the water's ability to support the pH, and to resist pH change. If you have ever tried to

Above: a group of Heckel discus. Note the pronounced ▶ fifth vertical stripe, the most characteristic feature of Heckel discus.
Below: An exquisite turquoise discus in lovely planted aquarium—the type of picture that draws aquarists to discus!

Water Chemistry and Filtration

lower the pH of an aquarium by using a "pH down" solution (or sodium bisulfate) only to find it bounce back up in a day or two, you have seen the buffering capacity of water hardness in action.

Usually the pH value of water is the result of the ratio between dissolved carbon dioxide and the carbonate hardness of the water. In the waters from which discus come, however, the presence of large amounts of humic acids and salts complicates the chemistry. Without either a sufficient amount of humus or water hardness, it is possible for the pH of very soft water to quickly fall as low as 4.5, a phenomenon known as "acid fall." Acid fall can result in the sudden death of expensive discus. For this reason and others already cited, it is probably a mistake to attempt to duplicate the extremely low hardness of Amazon waters in our aquariums.

We have mentioned that discus come from waters with hardness levels of often less than 1°dH. In these natural waters, in place of carbonates and bicarbonates, large amounts of humic acids and their salts control the pH. It is very difficult to duplicate the correct amount of humic acids and salts in the aquarium, however, and if you did, the water would be considerably discolored. At least 3–4°dH is required to maintain sufficient buffering capacity to prevent acid fall. Also, at least 3°dH is necessary to sustain the proper amount of carbon

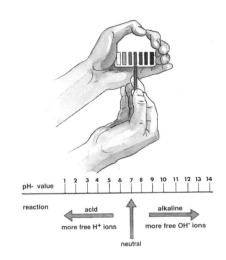

Using a color comparator test kit to determine pH. In this test, a strip is immersed in the aquarium, and the resulting color is compared with a color key. Colors on the key correspond with certain pH levels. Other test kits use liquid reagents, which are dissolved in a sample of aquarium water. Again, the resulting colors are compared with a color key supplied with the test.

dioxide necessary for optimal plant growth. Maintaining discus in a total water hardness of between 10–15°dH is a good compromise to reconcile the water hardness in the natural habitat, the aquarium appearance, and ease of maintenance. The pH should be maintained between 6 and 7. For breeding purposes, the pH should be lowered to between 5.5 and 6, and the total hardness between 7–10°dH.

Aquarists tend to pay too much attention to pH measurements. It is far more important to maintain the hardness of the aquarium water within acceptable limits. So long as you adjust the hardness of the water before it goes into the aquarium and do regular partial water changes, you should have little problem keeping the pH of your aquarium water within an acceptable range.

◄ Above left: The prominent fifth vertical stripe reveals this attractive fish to be a cross between a Heckel discus and a turquoise discus.
Above right: Red turquoise discus.
Below left: A red turquoise "crocodile" discus, so named because of the unusual scale pattern. The photographer has captured the iridescence of this fish exceptionally well. Note the small abrasion on this otherwise perfect fish. Such a small wound is easily treated, and the expense and effort involved in treatment are insignificant compared to the value of this fish.
Below right: A solid brilliant turquoise discus with exceptionally good coloration on the face and head.

The Oxygen Cycle

In tropical streams, dissolved oxygen is supplied through surface gas exchange, the photosynthesis of aquatic plants, and, in some places, by infusion of spring water. Observations have shown that dissolved oxygen levels rise as the day progresses, which is a sure indication that plant respiration, driven by photosynthesis through the light of the sun, causes dissolved oxygen levels to rise.

It is important to maintain high dissolved oxygen levels in the discus aquarium. Insufficient oxygen contributes to long-term stress and stunted growth and development. Most dissolved oxygen enters the aquarium at the water surface, so lack of surface film and good circulation within the aquarium are necessary to promote oxygen super-saturation in the aquarium. Much dissolved organic pollution consists of molecules described as surfactants which, because of their polar molecular structure, are attracted to an air/water interface, such as the water surface. This causes an oily film at the water surface, and such a film is a common cause of poor dissolved oxygen levels.

Dissolved oxygen levels in the aquarium can be tested by test kits. If dissolved oxygen levels in the aquarium are not near saturation after several hours of illumination, the reason must be found and eliminated. Common causes include insufficiently filtered water (which contributes to a surface film), lack of circulation within the aquarium, and insufficient plant growth (in planted aquariums).

During the day, when photosynthesis takes place, plants consume the carbon dioxide exhaled by fish and give off oxygen, which the fish consume.

At night, when photosynthesis does not take place, plants remove oxygen from the water and produce carbon dioxide. Fish also breath in oxygen and exhale carbon dioxide, so oxygen levels may be lower at night than during the day.

Getting Started

Placement of the Aquarium

Discus are very sensitive to vibrations and other disturbances. For this reason, give careful thought to the location of the aquarium. Do not place the aquarium in a high traffic area, such as a main hallway, a playroom, or a child's bedroom. Also, consider your activity patterns in the house, and do not put the discus aquarium in a room where the lights are often switched on and off. Even though the aquarium lighting may be on, the fish will be startled every time the room lights are switched on.

Placement on a ground floor is better than placement on an upper level, since the upper levels of the house will probably have more floor vibration than the ground floor. If you like listening to loud music on the stereo, you probably shouldn't place the aquarium near your loudspeakers. Positioning the aquarium in the corner of a room will subject it to less vibration than will placement in the middle of the room or against a single wall.

Examples of common aquarium shapes. Top: a tall "show" aquarium. Center: An acrylic aquarium with top bracing. Bottom: a traditional rectangular aquarium.

Discus seem very sensitive to movement above their heads. For this reason, the discus aquarium should not be located lower than waist level. Otherwise, the discus will be constantly subjected to motion above their heads which they cannot identify. Most discus breeders keep their aquariums at about the chest level of an average person.

The aquarium should not be placed where it will get direct sunlight. Direct sunlight can cause excessive algae growth, and your aquarium water will turn a very unattractive green color. True, the fish will probably love it, but we must please both fish and fishkeeper. Direct sunlight may also raise the water temperature to unacceptable levels, or make it difficult to regulate.

Necessary Equipment

Selecting a Good Retailer

If a retailer in your area does a good job with discus, be thankful. Even if you decide to purchase your discus stock through individual breeders or from mail order, you still need a good retailer for food, equipment, advice, and emergencies. Make a point of visiting all the tropical fish shops in your area, and be willing to drive a distance to find the right one. Look for a place with a knowledgeable staff who have time to listen to customers, and who will give you correct information even if it means losing a sale. Listen to the way the staff talk to their customers. Are they patient? Are they willing to special order products or fish for you? Do the fish in the shop appear healthy, and are the tanks clean? Do customers seem happy to be there, or are they having problems? A really good store is a "happening place," where people stop by just to have something to do. Try very hard to find a store like this.

The Aquarium and Canopy

The aquarium itself should be of good construction. The best shapes are still the traditional rectangles or cubes, for these allow the most surface area in relation to volume, the best viewing angles, and territorial area for fish. It is at the water's surface that oxygen enters the water, so the more surface area, the better chance your fish have at getting sufficient oxygen. Other shapes (such as hexagons) are workable, but the reduced surface area limits the fish-holding capacity of the aquarium. A warning about unusual shapes like hexagons: the distorted images produced by the angles are irritating to many people. Also, if a hexagon aquarium has not been carefully constructed, it is more prone to leakage than a cube or rectangle aquarium.

Discus are one of the few freshwater fish for which tall "show" aquariums are appropriate. Because most fish establish their territories based on bottom structures such as rocks and substrate, for them, an aquarium taller than about 15 inches (38 cm) is just wasted space. But because of the height of discus' bodies, and also because you may want to use submerged driftwood for aquascaping, taller aquariums are desirable for discus. For adult discus, the aquarium should be at least 18 inches (45.5 cm) tall. Get the largest aquarium you can afford. Many people make the mistake of starting out with small aquariums, thinking that they'll start small and work their way up. That's not the way to do it. As we've seen, it is easier to keep water chemistry stable in a larger volume of water. Look at it this way: a morsel of uneaten food rotting in a 20-gallon (75.6 L) aquarium will cause more of a problem than in a 75-gallon (284 L) aquarium. For this reason, a 55-gallon (208 L) aquarium—48" x 13" x 20" (123 cm x 33 cm x 50 cm)—is minimum size for a good discus aquarium. In an aquarium of this size, water quality will remain fairly stable, and the fish will have enough room to move around. Also, a 55-gallon (208 L) aquarium is still small enough to keep down filtration and heating costs.

The aquarium should be constructed of either acrylic or float (plate) glass. Be wary of aquariums made of tempered glass, which shatters when stressed and cannot be drilled for special filtration. If the aquarium is made of acrylic, be sure it has plenty of bracing around the top, particularly at the corners. Because of the flexibility of the material, acrylic aquariums need more bracing than glass aquariums. Acrylic also scratches much more easily than glass, so if you choose acrylic, be careful. Note that better acrylic aquariums often have fewer seams, because some of the corners are molded.

The Aquarium Stand

Structural Considerations: Be sure to place the aquarium on a stand that is strong, flat, and level. The stand must be able to support the weight of the aquarium, water, substrate, and decorative rocks. If the stand is not absolutely level, it may cause pressure cracks in the walls of the aquarium. If you are not completely sure that the stand is flat and level, put a sheet of 1/2-inch (1.2 cm) Styrofoam between the aquarium and the stand to level out any

Examples of common aquarium stands. Top Left: a wrought iron stand, inexpensive but not very stable or decorative. Top Right: A solid stand with storage shelves, but not much room for under-tank filtration equipment. Bottom Left: A solid stand with a door to conceal the abundant room for filtration equipment. Bottom Right: A solid stand for an octagonal or flatback hexagon aquarium.

inadequacies of the stand. Also, do not assume that the floor is level. Very often the aquarium stand may be of excellent construction, but if placed on a floor that is not level, the tank will still be in danger. Use plastic or wooden shims to level your stand before putting water in the aquarium, and make sure the shims are strong and securely in place!

Materials: Aquarium stands are available in many different materials. An acrylic stand is acceptable for an acrylic aquarium. Your best choice of materials is usually a solid wood stand. Solid wood stands are strong, attractive, and durable. Avoid stands made of particle board or other compressed woods, because they swell and warp when wet, and may eventually collapse or give rise to pressure cracks in the aquarium.

Custom Installations: More and more aquarists are choosing custom aquarium installations. If the aquarium is built into a wall or otherwise integrated with the interior design, the aquarium will be an asset to the room rather than just an ugly wet corner of an otherwise attractive room. In addition, furniture-grade aquarium cabinets are available in designer finishes.

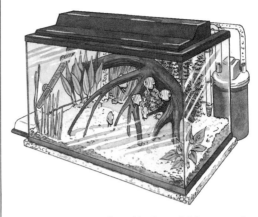

A planted discus aquarium with submersible heater, canister filter, and a large piece of decorative driftwood.

Type of Aquarium Setup

Standard Aquarium: A standard aquarium is a simple setup with undergravel filter, heater, thermometer, a gravel substrate, and some mechanical filter such as a canister or box filter. In a standard aquarium, plants, rocks, and often driftwood make up the decoration for the aquarium. This is certainly the most common, most simple, and least expensive type of discus aquarium.

Breeding Aquarium: If you intend to be a breeder, you will make a serious commitment of time, money, space, and organization. In a breeding situation, it is not practical to have an aquarium decorated with plants, rocks, and driftwood, and especially not with any other fish in the aquarium besides the breeding pair. Usually, the only items in a breeding tank beside the fish and the water is an airstone, heater, sponge filter, and a clay flowerpot on which the fish lay their eggs. Such a setup is practical, but not very aesthetic.

Planted Aquarium: A particularly fascinating way to maintain discus is in a planted aquarium, as it affords the fish an attractive, natural, healthful environment, while allowing you to mix other fish

An attractive custom-made discus aquarium with floating plants. Notice the aquascaping, with the taller plants in back and shorter plants in the foreground.

It is possible to integrate an attractive aquarium and related equipment into the room decor with a minimum of intrusion.

species with the discus. Also, the planted aquarium offers the aquarist a new aspect of the hobby to learn about—freshwater plants. See the next chapter, "The Planted Discus Aquarium."

Lighting

Discus come from waters that are a mix of filtered sunlight and shadows. At different times during the day discus move from brightly lit areas into places that are shaded by an overhanging bank or by floating plants. Sunlight doesn't penetrate far into the stained waters, but since discus stay in relatively shallow water, it is a mistake to say that discus should be kept only in dimly lit aquariums. Discus should be provided with the options of bright and shaded conditions.

When we speak of light for aquariums, we must consider its two major aspects, *intensity* and *spectrum*. By intensity we mean the total amount of visible light reaching a surface. Spectrum, on the

other hand, refers to the individual bands of light. Visible light is composed of many different bands of light. We are concerned with those bands of light that penetrate the water, causing the growth of aquatic plants and affecting the way fish perceive objects and are perceived by us.

For a breeding setup or for a fish-only aquarium, our only lighting concerns are enough intensity and the proper spectrum to display the fishes' coloration. This can easily be achieved with one, or, at the most, two common aquarium light fixtures, as long as we carefully choose the lamps.

The light source of choice will almost always be a fluorescent lamp. Fluorescent lamps are by far the most common types of lamp for aquariums, because they are inexpensive, easily replaced, give off very little heat, and are available in a wide variety. Incandescent lamps are usually not desirable for aquariums because of the tremendous heat they emit, and because incandescent lamps are very inefficient.

Efficiency is a measurement of the portion of electricity consumed by a lamp that is converted to visible light. Only about 6 percent of the electricity consumed by an incandescent lamp is converted to visible light. Fluorescent lamps are very efficient, converting upwards of 60 percent of the electricity consumed into visible light. This is why a 40-watt incandescent lamp burns much hotter than a 40-watt fluorescent lamp.

For displaying your discus, one or two fluorescent lamps with color temperature of around 5000°K and a Color Rendering Index (CRI) of around 90 will be ideal.

Heating

We have already seen that discus require higher temperatures than most other tropical fish. While it is true that discus can be maintained at temperatures of around 78°F (25.5°C), they thrive at 82°F (27.7°C)–88°F (31°C). Any other fishes or live plants kept in a discus aquarium must also be able to do well at these elevated temperatures.

The most common type of aquarium heater is the glass rod heater. Today, there is no reason to buy anything other than a fully submersible heater, which is so well sealed that no part of the heater must remain outside the water. Only a small opening in the aquarium canopy is needed for the heater cord. Submersible heaters are the safest, as they are well sealed and insulated. Don't forget to include an accurate thermometer for your aquarium. Many aquarium thermometers, unfortunately, are cheap and inaccurate. Money spent on a thermometer that will give you the aquarium's exact temperature is money well spent.

The role of an aquarium heater is not so much to initially heat the aquarium as it is to maintain a constant temperature. Stable temperatures are crucial for tropical fish. A quick drop of two to three degrees can trigger an outbreak of parasites, and constant temperature fluctuation will keep your fish under stress.

The heater must be of appropriate size. Two watts/gallon is the general standard. Thus, a 75-gallon aquarium would need a 150-watt heater. There are several advantages, however, to using two heaters, each with half the total needed wattage. With two 75-watt heaters, if one fails, the aquarium will still be heated. In a discus aquarium, where expensive fish need to be kept at very warm temperatures, the failure of your heater may cost you quite an investment, so it is probably worth the cost of a second heater. Another advantage of using two heaters is that if one happens to get stuck "on," as heaters occasionally do, it will take a 75-watt heater longer to cook your fish than it would a 150-watt model!

Beware of using only one heater with a capacity that is either too large or too small. An underpowered heater will stay on too long; the points of the heater may stick and cook your fish, or the heater might burn out prematurely. Conversely, an oversized heater will switch on and off too often and wear out, and if an oversized heater happens to stick on, the water will overheat very quickly.

There is another type of aquarium heater that is not often used, called a heating mat. Heating mats completely remove the heating element from the water, which eliminates any electrical hazard. Additionally, a heating mat warms the aquarium water evenly, as opposed to a glass rod heater, which heats the water in its vicinity and relies on currents within the aquarium to distribute the heat. Heating mats also eliminate the risk of a fish's being burned by a glass rod heater.

Cable heating is a method that is of particular value in a planted aquarium, so this is discussed in the next chapter, "The Planted Discus Aquarium."

Setting-Up Procedures

Before placing an aquarium on its stand, use a carpenter's level to see if the stand is level. It is likely that the floor is not quite level, so use small shims to level the stand before proceeding. Once the stand is level, put a sheet of 1/2 inch (1.2 cm) Styrofoam on top of the stand, and place the aquarium on the Styrofoam sheet. The Styrofoam might help prevent pressure cracks in case the stand is deficient. Leave at least 1 1/2 inches (3.8 cm) between the aquarium and the wall for filter hoses, electrical cords, and access in case anything falls (or jumps!) behind the aquarium.

Aquascaping

Many discus keepers have never learned to display their fish in a pleasing manner. While there may be reasons (such as the goal of breeding the fish) to keep discus in an unadorned aquarium, few aquarists will be satisfied with such an arrangement in their living rooms. The goal of aquascaping is to provide an environment for the aquarium inhabitants that simulates their natural habitat while presenting an attractive and functional display for the aquarist. Our earlier observations about the habitat of discus will help us choose aquascaping materials that achieve both goals.

Background Considerations: It is possible to build an elaborate scenic background out of cork, rock, or other materials, or you may choose a solid colored background of blue, black, or green. Some may choose a commercial scenic background, though some purists might blanch at the thought. Photographic backgrounds often draw attention to themselves and *away* from the fish. Remember that the fish often feel insecure unless they have the security of a background. If you are designing a "room divider" aquarium that is open from all four sides, you should provide enough cover in the center of the aquarium to satisfy the needs of your discus.

Substrate Considerations: Unlike many other cichlids, discus seldom disturb the substrate. You will probably purchase a commercial aquarium substrate, though large-particle sandblasting gravel is just as suitable, natural in appearance, and inexpensive. Look for the darker, natural gravels because these will not reflect light. Most aquarium gravel is quartz, and is perfectly acceptable for discus. River sand is also attractive, and is suitable so long as it does not contain calcium. If you are unsure about the mineral makeup of the substrate, put a little of the gravel in a cup with some vinegar or diluted hydrochloric acid. If the vinegar fizzes, the gravel contains calcium or other pH buffering minerals that slowly but surely will raise the carbonate hardness of your aquarium. Whichever substrate you purchase, buy enough to provide a suitable depth for your needs. If you are using undergravel filtration, a depth of 2 to 3 inches (5–7.5 cm) is about right, while if you are not using an undergravel filter, the danger of anaerobic contamination in the gravel restricts you to no more than 1 inch (2.5 cm) of substrate. Be sure to rinse the substrate in a bucket or strainer under tap water until the water runs clear.

Substrate Aesthetics: Do not lay the substrate in a flat, even layer across the bottom. It is usually best to slope the gravel downward from the back to the front. Sloping the gravel adds visual interest,

and it also channels detritus toward the front of the aquarium where it is easily removed. Gravel may be terraced by building barriers with panes of glass or plastic, which are cemented to the tank bottom. Unfastened terraces made with rocks and wood are less stable; the gravel tends eventually to level itself out. Use only silicone cement designed for aquariums, and allow 72 hours for it to completely cure. Many silicones purchased from hardware stores contain mildewcides that will poison the fish and beneficial bacteria, and uncured silicone contains compounds toxic to fish.

Rockwork Considerations: Rockwork is not the aquascaping essential for discus that it is with various other cichlids. If you do use decorative rock in your discus aquarium, selection is important, because many rocks (including many sold for aquarium use) contain metal ores or pH buffering minerals. Marble is a calcium derivative, and is thus unsuitable for discus. Only smooth, worn rocks should be used for discus. Avoid limestone and other rocks that will raise the alkalinity of your aquarium. Perform the vinegar test (as with substrate) on any rocks of unknown mineral content before putting them in your aquarium. Granite, quartzite, petrified wood, shale, and slate are safe for discus, though some may question the aesthetics of putting granite in a discus aquarium. Scrub all rocks before putting them in your aquarium, as many rocks hold sand, dirt, and even plant matter.

Rockwork Aesthetics: Keep rock decoration to a minimum, because there are other more significant aquascaping features in a discus aquarium. Discus do not need caves through which to swim or rocks to hide behind; too many rocks will spoil the aesthetics and function of a discus aquarium. Avoid too many types and colors of rocks. Remember that in nature similar types of rocks usually occur together. Therefore, it looks much more natural when just a few of only one type of rock are used. Smooth, dark rocks are the best choice for discus tanks.

Driftwood Considerations: Driftwood is often available from pet stores, and its use in discus aquariums is highly recommended. Driftwood, however, has several drawbacks. The most obvious is that it floats, though natural, untreated woods that are heavier than water are also on the market. Boiling driftwood or running hot water over it in a bathtub will help drive out the air and saturate the wood with water, though large pieces of wood may take significant exposure to water to become entirely saturated (sometimes up to six months). Driftwood from pet dealers comes attached to a slate bottom, but sometimes the slate is not heavy enough to hold the wood down, and sometimes the slate is so large that it obstructs a significant portion of the aquarium substrate. Cutting off the circulation of water through too much of the substrate will cause anaerobic pockets under the slate. A better choice is to silicone cement the wood directly to the bottom of the aquarium before putting in heating cables or substrate. Many types of driftwood will stain the aquarium water with tannin, which is harmless (and possibly even preferred) by the discus, since tannin is one element in the blackwater rivers in which discus are found. Eventually the wood will stop leaching out tannins, so frequent water changes and the use of activated carbon in the filter will soon eliminate the staining.

Driftwood Aesthetics: The most significant aquascaping feature of a discus aquarium can be waterlogged driftwood. You can do no better at simulating a normal discus habitat than to provide submerged driftwood, especially if you can get a stump with some roots intact that will fit within the width of your aquarium. The closest most of us will ever get to seeing discus in their natural state is to watch them glide between plants and the roots of a tree stump. The stump will also provide shade from the lighting. If you can't find a small enough stump to fit in your aquarium you can simulate the effect with several pieces of driftwood arranged together. Driftwood also provides an excellent place to anchor certain aquarium plants such as Java fern and Java moss. Limited amounts of tannin from the submerged wood give the water a natural

It is also possible to suspend branches from the aquarium molding (trim) so that they hang down into the water. Some aquarists have even gone so far as to design an elaborate construction where the stump rises up out of the aquarium, attached to which are branches that extend out across the water and drape partially downward into the water. Land plants are then placed among the exposed branches, some with their roots growing down into the water and extracting nutrients from the water. In this way the aquarium becomes not just a "fish tank," but a part of the ambiance of the room.

"blackwater" look that is considered pleasing by many aquarists.

Plant Considerations: Many will argue that plastic plants have no place in a "real" aquarium, but your choice between live and plastic plants depends on how involved you want to get with the aquarium. The cultivation of live aquarium plants can be an interesting aspect of the hobby, but you can achieve an attractive display with lifelike plastic plants. Almost all plastic plants available in pet stores today are safe and colorfast.

Plant Aesthetics: If you choose plastic plants, please avoid fluorescent colors. These are not appropriate for a discus aquarium, because the discus themselves furnish spectacular color. Select plants in natural hues of brown, red, and green. Pick out at least a few plants as tall as the aquarium. Shorter plants look nice in the foreground. Don't arrange your plants in an "orderly" fashion, with an alternating pattern of red, brown, and green! The aquarium will look more natural if you place bunches of similar plants together. Such an arrangement will render the most natural appearance possible.

Preparation of Tap Water

Tap water contains the necessary trace elements for fish and plant growth. We do not use 100 percent distilled water for discus because it is devoid of essential trace elements, making it impossible to maintain a stable pH.

For years chlorine has been put in municipal water to kill bacteria. For this we must be grateful, but chlorine is death to both beneficial aquarium bacteria and the fish. Fortunately, chlorine is easy to eliminate. Chlorine is a gas, and it will rise out of solution if we simply let the water stand overnight. But there is no need to wait, because many commercial preparations immediately neutralize free chlorine in tap water.

Chlorine has one drawback for water purification—it sometimes combines with dissolved organic substances to form carcinogenic trihalomethane. For this reason most municipal water supplies are no longer treated with free chlorine, but with chloramine, a much more insidious chemical for aquarium fauna. Chloramine is formed by combining ammonia (NH_3) with chlorine. This combination forms a very stable bond that breaks down only with a high dose of sodium thiosulfate. Unfortunately, when the bond is broken, the ammonia is released, which is almost as bad as chlorine for fish. Commercial dechlorination preparations do not rid the aquarium of chloramine. They simply break the bond between chlorine and ammonia, and rely on the filtration devices in your aquarium to process or adsorb the ammonia. Chloramine is toxic to fish at levels above .05 mg/L, but it is commonly present in tap water at levels exceeding 1.0 mg/L. Fortunately, there are now commercial preparations that effectively deal with chloramine. If your water supply contains chloramine, be certain that you purchase a chloramine remover. A simple dechlorinator will not do the job.

After insuring that your tap water is safe from chloramine and chlorine, adjust the hardness (if necessary) to an acceptable level. This is easy to do in an initial installation, as you need only test your tap water and add the necessary amount of deionized water. Alternatively, you can simply fill your entire aquarium with tap water and soften the entire water volume through peat until you reach the desired level of hardness.

Initial Conditioning of the Aquarium

After the aquarium has been filled with dechlorinated water of the correct hardness, the biological conditioning of the water begins. This involves culturing a sufficient quantity of nitrifying bacteria for the fish load of the aquarium. Start the water circulation through the biological (undergravel, box, or canister) filter, and set the heater temperature up to 88°F (31°C). The bacteria will multiply faster in the warmer water. Let the water circulate through the filters for about a day, giving the water time to reach the desired temperature. Also, check all air and water hoses for leaks.

The easiest way to introduce both bacteria and nitrogen products is to put a handful of hardy fish in the aquarium and let them eat. The fish bring small amounts of nitrifying bacteria with them on their bodies, and as the fish excrete waste they provide nitrogen wastes for the bacteria to consume. When the fish excrete ammonia, the ammonia level of the aquarium water rises, because the ammonia is building up faster than the bacteria can consume it. Testing the water with an ammonia test kit reveals this gradual buildup of ammonia. After the *Nitrosomonas* bacteria have built up to sufficient levels, the ammonia level will fall, and the nitrite level will begin to rise. Again, this is because the second type of nitrifying bacteria, *Nitrobacter* sp., have not yet built up to levels sufficient to process the nitrite as it is produced by the *Nitrosomonas* sp. At such a time as the *Nitrobacter* sp. have reached a sufficient level, nitrite levels will fall to nothing. When both ammonia and nitrite levels reach zero, the aquarium is said to be conditioned, or to have "cycled."

For the first week after fish have been introduced, test the ammonia every other day. During the second and third weeks, test both ammonia and nitrite every other day. Record the test results so you can see the progression of the conditioning. After the aquarium has cycled, test the pH and general hardness, and do a 20 percent water change with hardness-adjusted water. Alternatively, you could simply put a few fish in the aquarium and begin testing for nitrite after 2 weeks.

Which fish should you use for conditioning? Many aquarists may want to use a few festivums, because these come from the discus' native waters, and because the plan may be to keep festivums with the discus anyway. It is also possible to purchase commercial solutions for biologically conditioning aquarium water. These preparations contain nitrifying bacteria in suspension, and also contain a food for the bacteria. If you choose to use such a preparation, carefully follow the directions supplied with the product, as failure to follow the directions explicitly can cause nitrite levels to reach extremely high levels, and may require several large water changes to dilute the nitrite.

Selecting Good Discus

Wild-Caught or Tank-Bred?

As a general rule, wild-caught fish are best left to experts and breeders, so most discus keepers should direct their attentions toward the captive-raised strains. This is because captive-raised specimens have been acclimated to domestic water supplies and the acceptance of prepared foods. Captive-raised discus are also somewhat more resistant to the most common aquarium diseases, since they have been exposed to common aquarium ailments for generations. With wild-caught discus, you must gradually acclimate them to the harder water and higher pH in which they will probably be kept, and you must patiently get them to start feeding on foods that are available to you.

If you do purchase wild-caught discus, you may want to quarantine them or keep them for the first few weeks with some disease-free festivums or angelfish. Frozen bloodworms or whiteworms are very useful in getting wild-caught discus to start eating, as are live brine shrimp.

Health

The first step to success is obtaining healthy fish. Look for fish that are active and robust looking—not fish that cower in the corner or seem intimidated by their tankmates. Notice the forehead of the fish. It should be full and broad, not pinched and skinny. Thinness in the forehead is a sure indication of malnutrition or internal worms. A shrunken abdomen indicates that the fish has gone a while without food and may refuse to eat, but some thinness of the abdomen area is tolerable if the fish's forehead is filled out and the fish is eating. Check to make sure the body profile is round, because many poorer-quality discus have lost their natural roundness of body. Notice whether the size of the eye appears to be in proper proportion to the rest of the body. If the eye looks too large, the fish is stunted and will never grow into a healthy adult.

Obviously, don't buy a fish that has body lesions. The lesion can probably be treated and cured, but treatment becomes more difficult when accompanied by the normal stress of acclimation. The dealer is in a better position to treat the injury, because he doesn't need to transport and acclimate the fish as you would have to do.

Discus that are dark and show their vertical bands are excited or under severe stress. You must determine whether the cause is serious. Don't consider buying a small fish with unusually bright coloration, which probably indicates that the fish has been treated with hormones. Such fish may lose their color and be sterile. Avoid fish that are obviously in distress—doing a "headstand" or "tailstand" in the corner. Notice whether any white strings of feces hang from the fish's vent. This is usually an indication of disease, and the fish (and possibly all fish in that tank) should be declined.

Be certain to watch the fish feed. Notice whether they aggressively attack the food, or pick at it and spit it out. Discus that pick at their food may become excellent specimens after careful attention, but if you are paying full price, you should expect an excellent specimen from the start. Notice whether the fish seems to have difficulty locating the food. Some discus seem to have difficulty focusing their vision at close range; this appears to be an inbred vision defect that they never overcome. It is not blindness. These fish come rushing over to the food when it hits the water, so they obviously can see, but if the food is sinking they strike below it, and if the food is on the bottom they hit behind it. They repeatedly try to feed but cannot focus precisely on the food. These fish live through exportation because at their hatcheries in the Far East the fish are commonly fed large masses of live tubifex worms, so the fish has a fair chance of striking the food. On smaller servings of food, as in the home aquarium, the fish cannot feed properly and are soon malnourished. Such fish will always have trouble competing for sufficient food, and will never reach their full potential. This vision defect has been noticed in fish as small as a nickel. Therefore, ask to see a discus feed on pellets or some other small food particles. Since this vision problem is genetic, such fish, if they survive to maturity, should not be used for breeding stock.

On adult discus, examine the head carefully for pits and lesions. These are usually indications of an environmental problem, and while it can be reversed and treated, there is no reason to purchase a fish with problems. Notice whether the fish breathes out of only one set of gills at a time. A fish that breathes with one gill plate flared and the other clamped shut almost surely has gill flukes, which can be treated, but which may already have done severe damage to sensitive tissues.

Fish suspected of having been dosed with hormones should be rejected outright. The practice is deceptive, destructive, and despicable. Hormone-influenced discus are in a class with the artificially "painted glass fish" that are so often seen in pet stores

Size

You will usually be offered discus in one of three sizes: juvenile ("quarter size"), adolescent ("half dollar size"), and adult. In adult fish you should expect to see full color and development. Look for a bright red eye and a wide forehead when viewed from the front. Because you should expect to pay a premium for quality adult discus, do not purchase them from a distant dealer you don't know. Only by your inspecting the fish and observing their behavior and eating habits can you be assured of getting your money's worth. If these are your first discus, or if you have yet to be successful at keeping discus, it is better to buy smaller, less expensive fish and grow them to adult size.

"Half-dollar-size" fish should show the beginning of adult coloration, and these are the largest fish you should expect to order from a distant dealer. Dealers will sell large adults and even breeding pairs, but large discus do not ship well, so there is always the increased chance of shipping stress and damage. If you purchase half-dollar-size fish, about six or eight of them will be right to establish a breeding colony.

"Quarter-size" fish are usually about three months old. Such fish are the easiest to ship by air freight, so if you are purchasing your fish from a distant dealer, this is probably the best size to get. A group of about ten quarter-size discus is about right to ensure that they feel safe in their new surroundings. Six is about the right number to buy if you want to ensure getting at least one breeding pair.

Conformation

Good quality discus possess the natural rounded shape. Avoid discus with pointed faces, or those that seem to be developing a "roman nose" or a "cichlid hump." These are traits that have been bred into discus by breeders who have not been selective enough about their breeding stock. Though there are certainly some strains of discus with higher dorsal fins than others, the round, thick body that is typical of wild discus is the standard, and this standard should be maintained by conscientious breeders and keepers everywhere.

Sexual Distinctions

It is impossible to sex juvenile discus. It is almost as difficult to sex adults, because discus cannot be sexed reliably according to external characteristics. It is possible to make an intelligent guess, however, based on observation. In general, males are larger and more thickly set than females, and the dominant fish in a group is usually a male. Among siblings, the male fish are usually larger than the females. Sometimes male discus show more pointed anal and dorsal fins than do females, and sometimes males have thicker lips than females do. There are no firm rules, however, so the sex of your fish cannot be reliably determined until a spawning pair forms. Often breeders who are familiar with their own particular strains can sex their fish based on experience.

Acclimation

Transportation

It is not objectionable for a group of small discus to be put together in one bag, though one fish per bag is better. Adult discus, however, should never be together in a bag, as their spines will punch holes in each other and serious infection can result. The fish should be double bagged (adults triple bagged) with newspaper between the bags to prevent their being punctured. The bag should be large enough to hold sufficient water to cover the fish and also large enough to hold two parts air to one part water. Yes, there should be more air than water in the bag. Ask your dealer to fill the bag with oxygen instead of room air if he's equipped to do so, and also ask for a Styrofoam box to transport the fish in. If you are buying more than one fish, a box is warranted, and Styrofoam will help insulate the water and keep it warm. Get a cover for the box so that the bright sunlight doesn't startle the fish and cause them to thrash around.

Acclimation

Wild-caught discus are removed from their native waters and stored at the exporter's facilities, where water changes often introduce polluted, bacteria-infested water from nearby wells. Amazingly, the drinking water for humans in these locales is sometimes less safe than the river water from which the discus come! They arrive at the dealer having spent days in this polluted water, and are immediately transferred into harder water with a much higher pH. This accounts for much of the stress and disease of wild-caught discus in pet stores. If you purchase wild-caught discus, it is critical that you gradually acclimate these fish to more familiar conditions.

Quarantine

All new discus, especially wild-caught ones, should be given a three week quarantine to disinfect them. It is important for you to be able to observe them for signs of disease, and for you to treat the aquarium with preventive medication whether or not you see any outward signs of disease. In addition, any fish intended to be kept with discus should also go through a separate quarantine period.

New discus will be jittery if you do not provide sufficient shelter for them to hide in. Ironically, the thicker and more abundant shelter you provide for fish, the more time they will spend out in full view, while if you provide little or no shelter, the fish will cower in the corner (the only refuge they can find). Procedures for acclimation and quarantine are described in the chapter "Disease Recognition and Treatment."

The Planted Discus Aquarium

A Brief Excursion into the Larger World of Fishkeeping

Part of our fishkeeping urge comes from the desire to bring a bit of nature into our homes. By keeping fish we inject a bit of the wild into our climate-controlled homes.

But keeping fish in an aquarium with purple gravel, plastic plants, and a ceramic "No Fishin' " sign doesn't resemble nature very much, does it? It is possible to create an authentic suggestion of a natural freshwater habitat in your home.

One of the most beautiful is the so-called "Dutch aquarium," where the aquarium is literally an underwater garden of plants. In contrast to the aquarium that has one or two struggling live plants mixed among plastic plants, Dutch aquariums are densely planted forests of red, green, and brown hues. In such aquariums it is not unusual for the plants to grow up out of the aquarium and into the rest of the room, often flowering above and on the surface of the aquarium water. Dutch aquariums are often so beautiful that the fish are noticed by viewers only as an afterthought, but the fish population in Dutch aquariums is as carefully considered as the plants.

It is possible to keep discus in a modified Dutch aquarium, as long as plants are chosen that thrive in the warm water that discus require. Compatible companion fish may also be added. Surely, keeping highly-colored discus in a densely-planted aquarium is the apex of the freshwater fishkeeping hobby!

Reasons for a Planted Aquarium

There are reasons to keep discus in a planted aquarium besides the obvious aesthetic advantage. Plants greatly aid in providing good water quality for your discus. Through their photosynthesis, plants provide a high level of dissolved oxygen during the day, when the fish are most active, and the roots of plants supply enough oxygen to the substrate to keep it from going anaerobic. Through

their uptake of minerals, plants (particularly the fast-growing species) also help prevent the hardness of the water from rising. Plants remove enough nitrogen compounds from aquarium water to be considered a "natural filter," and plants also provide shaded areas in the aquarium, so discus are free to move from "sunlight" to shadow. And live plants provide a habitat that at least somewhat resembles a natural one for the fish. Live plants provide numerous spawning sites for discus; they will attach their eggs to plants (as well as to driftwood, rocks, flower pots, or plastic plants). You may also notice that the discus' bright coloration seems even more intense in a planted aquarium. Reasons for keeping discus in a planted aquarium abound, but the greatest reason may be to extend your interest from being a fishkeeper to being an aquarist. It is easy to become more interested in the plants than in the fish!

The Proper Perspective

Remember, however, that the primary purpose of the discus aquarium is the successful maintenance of these fish, and all elements of the aquarium must promote this goal. For instance, certain species of catfish are helpful for controlling algae, but if these catfishes also have a taste for the mucus on the sides of discus, these catfishes are obviously out. Or, there may be a kind of plant that you would love to keep in your aquarium, but it needs cooler temperatures than discus will tolerate. Lowering the water temperature for the plant could have disastrous consequences for your discus.

We will discuss some advanced techniques for keeping aquarium plants. It behooves us to remember, however, that years ago beautiful planted aquariums were kept without benefit of the devices we will describe. A successful planted discus aquarium can be kept with just substrate, a heater, and proper lighting. All other devices are simply tools for doing the job more efficiently, or in a more automated fashion. Use of advanced techniques and equipment virtually guarantees success to the layperson, and makes difficult plants easier for the expert to maintain, but is by no means necessary for an attractive planted aquarium.

The Substrate

Of particular importance is the substrate. Typically, aquarium substrates are used with undergravel filters as biological filters, or the substrates are kept as clean as possible and used as anchors and decoration for the bottom of the aquarium. For plants, however, the substrate is of primary importance for nutrition and rooting. The roots of live plants require slightly anaerobic ("without oxygen") conditions to thrive. The substrate must not be totally anaerobic, or the roots will rot and the substrate will become a pollution factory. The substrate must also be able to hold iron-rich nutrients for rooted plants. In tropical streams the substrate is a repository of such nutrients. Soil-bound minerals are found in the chemical form the plants can utilize. In an aquarium, if too much oxygen from the water circulates through the substrate, the minerals are oxidized into compounds that are no longer useful to plants. Because of the highly aerobic (oxygenated) conditions caused by an undergravel filter, and because an undergravel filter would simply "wash out" any fertilizer from the substrate, undergravel filters should not be used for planted aquariums.

Substrate Heating

In the tropics the soil tends to be slightly warmer than the surrounding water. Because warm water rises, the greater warmth in the soil causes slight convection circulation between the soil and the water, just enough to keep the soil from going completely anaerobic, but not so that the roots of the plants are over-oxygenated. In a typical aquarium, the heater is in the water, far away from the substrate, so the substrate is slightly cooler than the aquarium water. This condition simply is not best for aquatic plants. Fortunately, there is a simple way

for us to simulate the thermal conditions of the tropical soil in our aquariums.

Low-voltage cable heating, buried in the aquarium substrate, enables us to make the gravel slightly warmer than the aquarium water. This also helps circulate some water through the substrate to prevent it from going anaerobic. If you have ever seen a portion of an aquarium substrate turn black, if you have seen bubbles rising up out of the gravel, or if you have ever detected that "rotten-egg" smell in an aquarium, you have seen the effects of an anaerobic reaction, in which nitrate is reduced to more harmful nitrite, and hydrogen sulfide, the gas with the "rotten-egg" smell, is produced. Hydrogen sulfide is a highly toxic compound; it will kill fish as well as plants if an anaerobic reaction is allowed to run unchecked. Substrate cable heating will ensure a continuous slow circulation of nutrients and oxygen between the substrate and the aquarium water.

Because cable heating is low voltage, even if the integrity of the cables is breached, the electrical leakage into the aquarium is low enough so that it will not harm either your fish or you if you put your hand into the aquarium! The low-voltage aspect of cable heating thus makes it even more safe than the traditional glass immersion heater, and it is impossible for the temperature to rise too high or for the fish to burn themselves against cable heating.

An electronic control maintains water temperature via an immersible temperature sensor. Cable heating requires a transformer to reduce the voltage, a control, and enough heating cable to cover the entire bottom of the aquarium. For this reason, cable heating is expensive—prohibitively expensive for many aquarists. Though there is no finer system than cable heating, and though you should use cable heating if you can justify the expense, there exists a lower-cost alternative that furnishes many of the benefits of cable heating for a fraction of the cost. It is possible to use a heating mat to achieve virtually the same effect as cable heating. Rubber heating mats adhere to the *outside* of the bottom glass panel of the aquarium. The heating mat warms the bottom glass panel, which in turn heats the substrate. Outside heating mats are not as efficient as immersed heating cables, but they do work, and for significantly less money than heating cables. Attached to the heating mat is an electronic control, and an immersible heat sensor is attached to the control with a waterproof cord. The heat sensor is put into the aquarium water with a suction cup, and the control automatically maintains the water temperature within a fraction of a degree. Because the heat source is nearer to the substrate than to the water, the substrate is always 2 to 3 degrees warmer than the water.

An advantage of heating mats is that no electronic components are in the water, thus all but eliminating electrical hazard. A disadvantage is that the mats are less efficient and therefore consume more electricity than either heating cables or glass immersion heaters.

Substrate Fertilization

In the tropics, water plants grow in iron-rich soils, so the plants are adapted to the nutrients found in those soils. Gravel additives (sometimes called "laterite") are available from several manufacturers in a clay, powdered, or granular form. These gravel additives are rich in iron and other fertilizers which are necessary for optimal growth of most tropical aquarium plants. The gravel additive you choose should be mixed with aquarium gravel of two to three millimeters size according to the ratio recommended by its manufacturer. Mix the gravel additive with washed, slightly damp gravel in a bucket, and place the mixture on the bottom of the aquarium in a layer from 3/4 inch (1.9 cm) to 1 inch (2.5 cm) deep if using heating cables. Add a layer of washed aquarium gravel of about the same depth on top of the bottom layer of fertilized gravel. This top layer will hold the fertilizer in the soil, and will look more attractive than the darker bottom layer. Fertilizer in tablet form is often packaged with the gravel additive, and these tablets should be inserted in the gravel near the roots of the major plants after they have been planted.

If you are using a heating mat, keep the gravel substrate no deeper than 1 1/2 inches (3.8 cm), because heating mats are not as effective as heating cables at evenly heating the substrate. If you use a heating mat and make your substrate too deep, the substrate may develop anaerobic pockets, which pollute the substrate and the water.

Lighting

For the planted aquarium the proper lighting is very important for the growth of healthy plants and prevention of excess algae.

Light, especially the bands of light known as PAR (Photosynthetically Active Radiation) light, drives photosynthesis. Photosynthesis is the process whereby plants synthesize carbohydrates (mostly glucose) from water and carbon dioxide through specialized pigment cells called chlorophyll, which are excited by various bands of light between 400–700 nanometers (PAR), depending on the particular type of chlorophyll pigments and accessory pigments present in the plant. Plants derive most of their food through photosynthesis—in fact, the reason most plant leaves are shallow and flat is in order to collect as much light as possible.

Just how much light does a planted aquarium need? Field observations have shown that most plants can grow within a range of divergent light

Above: A breeding pair of blue discus. Note the round ▶ profile characteristic of quality discus.
Below left: A brown discus in a breeding aquarium.
Below right: A domestic discus that was probably "color fed" with prawn eggs *(Macrobrachium rosenbergi)* or treated with hormones. Such fish show excessive reddish pigment in the soft tissues around the mouth and eye, and around the base of the pectoral fin and peduncle. These fish lose the enhanced coloration soon after being deprived of the hormone or color food.

The Planted Discus Aquarium

levels, because factors other than light intensity are significant in affecting plant growth.

The best measurement of light intensity for aquarium purposes is the *lumen*. As a general rule, a densely planted aquarium requires between 120 – 200 lumens per gallon (30 –50 lumens per liter) of water. This is probably a higher lumen figure than you are accustomed to, but we are looking for light levels that cause plants to thrive, not simply survive.

Commonly-seen rules about watts per gallon are flawed, because the amount of illumination per watt varies with the type of light source used. For example, you get many more lumens per watt from a metal halide lamp than from a fluorescent lamp, and you get more lumens per watt from some fluorescent lamps than others. Keep in mind that, as a general rule, the lumen measurement at the water surface will decrease by as much as 96 percent by the time it reaches the substrate of a 22-inch (56 cm) deep aquarium. The photoperiod (duration of light) should be from 10 –12 hours at the recommended light levels. Longer periods are not necessary and will needlessly encourage excess algae growth, while shorter periods are not sufficient for healthy plant growth. It is important for both your fish and plants to have a consistent photoperiod, so use of a timer on your lighting is highly recommended.

Fluorescent Lighting

The large majority of aquarists use fluorescent lighting for aquariums. Fluorescent lighting is energy efficient, lasts a long time, and runs much cooler than incandescent lighting, and it is a satisfactory light source for a planted aquarium.

Reflectors: Our goal is to get both the proper spectrum and intensity of light over the aquarium.

◄ A brown discus variant called the "half moon" discus. This is an interesting mutation that never really caught on in the hobby—possibly because of the prominent hump on the head and the high dorsal fin.

Intensity is a function of both the lumen output of the lamp and of the reflector that is used with the lamp. The importance of the reflector cannot be overemphasized, as a high quality reflector can squeeze lots of light out of even a mediocre lamp. The best reflectors are integrated with light fixtures to get the most light output. Look for a fixture with a high quality reflector and a lens to keep moisture away from electrical components.

The best reflectors are made out of specular aluminum, a highly-reflective material that does not absorb PAR value light. Many reflective materials seem to reflect light well, but unknown to the human eye the reflector absorbs some of the critical PAR value light you are trying to get to your plants.

Lamp Selection: In addition to the intensity of the light, it is also important to get the proper spectrum of light for the plants. The PAR spectrum includes the blue and violet bandwidths, which do not appear very bright to human eyes. These are the bandwidths, however, that "appear" brightest to plants. What is needed is a lamp or combination of lamps that provide both the PAR spectrum plants need and the yellow/green band width human eyes need to correctly perceive color, and it must present these bandwidths in a proper proportion.

Most "full spectrum" and "plant grow" lamps do not give the aquarium a natural appearance. Contrary to what you might think, "full spectrum" lamps that seek to "reproduce sunlight" usually are not able to also provide the color rendering of daylight. Therefore, most "full spectrum" lamps should also be avoided.

The common categories of color temperature are warm white (around 3600°K), white (around 4200°K), daylight (around 5000°K), and cool white (around 6000°K). As a rule, lamps with cold color temperatures (6000°K) cause plants to grow shorter and bushier, while lamps with warm color temperatures (3600°K) cause plants to grow tall and spindly. Lamps with a color temperature of around 5000°K are about ideal. You may rest the lights directly on the aquarium molding, but you may want to consider suspending the lighting above the aquarium, and removing the full glass canopy to allow your plants to grow up out of the aquarium. You will have the benefit of a new viewing angle on your aquarium, and you will be able to enjoy seeing your plants bloom and flower at the water's surface. Also, with an open top, feeding is simplified. Disadvantages include fish jumping out of the aquarium and heat loss from increased evaporation. If you choose to suspend the light above the aquarium, suspend fluorescent lights no higher than 12 inches (30.7 cm) above the water's surface.

HID (High Intensity Discharge) Lighting

HID lighting includes metal halide (HQI) and mercury vapor (HQL) lighting Both of these are high intensity light sources, and are excellent for plant growth, algae control, and good color rendition in the aquarium. HID lighting "punches" light much deeper into the aquarium than fluorescent lighting, so if you have an aquarium deeper than 24 inches (61 cm), some type of HID lighting may be right for you. HID light sources provide more lumens per watt than fluorescent lighting, and a typical HID lamp lasts significantly longer than a fluorescent tube. HID lighting, however, is more expensive to set up. Because of its longer effective life, however, in the long run HID lighting is less expensive than fluorescent.

Unlike fluorescent lighting, which evenly illuminates the aquarium, HID light sources are "spotlights," so they allow you to accentuate specific areas of the aquarium. HID lighting is also more easily suspended above the aquarium for the open top we have advocated for the planted aquarium.

It should be noted that all HID lighting must be used carefully. HID lamps were originally designed for outdoor use, and they generate quite a bit of heat. HID lamps should always be enclosed in a metal fixture with a 1/4 inch (.6 cm) glass (not tempered glass) lens. Aluminum is the preferred housing

material, as it is impervious to rust and corrosion, and dissipates heat well.

HID lighting almost always must be suspended some distance above the aquarium because of the heat generated by the light sources. Because of their intensity, HID lights are often suspended as much as 30 inches (77 cm) above the aquarium, depending on wattage and the particular application. When working on your aquarium, be aware that the housing of an HID lamp often gets hot enough to cause a severe burn if you brush against it.

Mercury vapor lighting is widely used in Europe for planted aquariums. A single 250-watt mercury vapor lamp will cast 13,000 lumens of light upon the surface of the aquarium water. Only a large, deep aquarium requires a 250-watt light. Mercury vapor lamps tend to cast a yellowish light, so you should select a phosphor coated lamp in an NDL (Near Daylight) finish. This phosphor coating will correct the lamp to a more suitable color rendition.

Metal halide lighting is the ultimate in HID lighting. Metal halide lamps provide the most lumens per watt of any adequate light source, and they render a very good color appearance. A 175-watt metal halide is ample unless you have an unusually large aquarium. Again, as with mercury vapor, an NDL phosphor coated lamp is best. Some specifications now include color temperatures of HID lamps; look for lamps between 4100–5500°K. A 175-watt metal halide lamp should be suspended at least 18 inches (45.5 cm) above the aquarium. With either mercury vapor or metal halide lighting, your plants will flourish, and your aquarium will become a luxuriant garden.

Discus, however, don't like constant bright light, so if you choose to use an HID lighting source, you must have enough plant growth (especially floating plants) to afford the discus some shady places. This option can easily be achieved by locating the HID light source off center, so if you have a 4-foot (1.2 m) long aquarium, hang the HID lamp only 1 foot (30.5 cm) from an end of the aquarium.

Algae Control

When a planted aquarium is set up it has a marked tendency toward algae growth. This is because of an abundance of light and nutrients.

Algae Control through Lighting

Fluorescent "grow lights" promote the growth of algae, especially during this initial phase. For this reason you should never use "plant lights," "grow lights," or "full spectrum" lighting on a plant aquarium until it has successfully been established for at least four months. Use of proper lamps during the initial phase of the aquarium will allow the fastest-growing plants to quickly extract nutrients and gain the advantage over algae.

Algae Control through Nutrient Competition

Algae and other aquarium plants are competitors. They compete for light and nutrients. Certain plants are known for rapid growth, and this rapid growth is a result of rapid uptake of phosphate, nitrate, and other plant nutrients that are especially abundant in a new aquarium. For this reason, a significant strategy for algae control is to initially plant the aquarium with a large quantity of these fast-growing plants. Examples of such plants are *Rotala* sp., *Vallisneria* sp., *Sagittaria* sp., and *Hygrophila* sp. Also, duckweed (*Lemna* sp.) grows extremely rapidly, and is thus an excellent tool for the prevention of algae problems. Duckweed, however, is a surface plant and can block light required by other plants if allowed to reproduce unchecked. Hardy, fast-growing plants quickly established in the aquarium will extract nutrients before algae have time to take over the aquarium, and will also quickly get their roots into the substrate, releasing oxygen and preventing the substrate from decaying. The key is to plant the aquarium densely from the very start. It is better to fill the aquarium with hardy, fast-growing plants and later thin them out to make room for other, possibly more desirable species. For example, the highly prized *Cryptocorynes* do not do well in an aquarium until it has been established for at least three months, and *Cryptocorynes* are almost totally unable to assimilate nitrate. Remember also that these plants suffer in bright light. Do not be a cheapskate on aquarium plants; it is better to spend more money on the plants and less money on filtration, because a dense growth of plants is the most significant filtration element in a planted aquarium. Many aquarists also allow the roots of certain potted land plants (such as philodendrons) to grow down into their aquariums in order to reduce nitrate and phosphate, and this concept can be taken a step further by building into the aquarium filtration system a culture of land plants through which the aquarium water constantly seeps. Significant reduction of nitrate and phosphate can be accomplished by this means.

Algae Control through Community Fish

Another strategy for algae control is to put several algae-eating fish in the planted aquarium at the very beginning, even if you don't care for the particular fish and do not intend to keep them indefinitely. After the first three months you may remove some, but not all, of the fish.

An excellent fish for control of algae is the flying fox, *Epalzeorhynchus siamensis*. *Ancistrus* catfishes are particularly adept at keeping submerged bogwood and roots clear of algae, but some discus keepers have had problems with *Ancistrus* sp. having a taste for the mucus secreted by the discus' skin. *Otocinclus affinis* is a small, shy, sucker-mouthed fish that does fairly well in a planted aquarium. The *Otocinclus* should be kept in a group of at least six to feel comfortable. They are too small to rely on them as your sole means of algae control, but a virtue of *Otocinclus* is that they are very compatible with discus. Note that the most common *Otocinclus* in the aquarium trade, *Otocinclus vittatus*, is the least hardy and least helpful member of its genus. A pair of dwarf gourami (*Colisa lalia*) are attractive fish that mix well with discus and are helpful in nibbling on algae, but they will occasionally also nibble on leaves of the more delicate plants. In a healthy planted aquarium, however, this damage is usually tolerable. *Hypostomus* sp. are commonly thought of as "algae eaters" for aquariums, but they are very damaging to plants and should not be considered. Neither should *Gyrinocheilus aymonieri* (Chinese algae eater) be used in the planted aquarium, as it eats less algae and becomes more aggressive and territorial as it matures.

Algae Control through Water Quality

Most algal problems result from poor water quality. If your water is too high in nitrate or phosphate, algae will thrive. If you use reverse osmosis or deionized water for water changes and evaporation top up, phosphate and nitrate will not become concentrated in your aquarium. Use of molecular adsorption resins for continuous chemical filtration also reduces phosphate. The main soluble nutrient for aquarium plants should be iron, not nitrate or phosphate. Kits for testing phosphate and nitrate are sold in aquarium shops.

Plant Nutrition

In nature, most nutrients critical for water plants are found in the soil, and other less chemically stable nutrients (mostly iron, manganese, nitrogen, and carbon) constantly leach out of the banks and into the water, where they are either quickly used up by plants or oxidized into forms that are unavailable to plants.

While tap water certainly contains many essential trace elements and other plant nutrients, these almost always occur in improper proportions, and other key plant nutrients are entirely absent from tap water. There is a detrimental surplus of some plant nutrients in tap water (especially phosphate), that often cause an overabundance of algae in aquariums.

Carbon Dioxide

Carbon is an essential nutrient for plants. Plants get most of their carbon from dissolved carbon dioxide in the water, but if sufficient free carbon dioxide is not present in the water, plants are able to extract carbon from bicarbonates in the water. This process is called biogenic decalcification, and certain plants can biogenically decalcify water enough to significantly lower the carbonate hardness of the water. It is important, therefore, to maintain sufficient carbon dioxide in the water to prevent plants from lowering the carbonate hardness of the water below the levels acceptable for maintenance of discus in a planted aquarium (10–15°KH). As a general rule, the higher the carbonate hardness, the more carbon dioxide required to maintain healthy equilibrium. Adequate carbon dioxide levels are therefore necessary in a densely planted aquarium.

It is necessary to test your aquarium water to determine whether the carbon dioxide levels are adequate. Test kits are available, and periodic testing for CO_2 is critical. It is possible to purchase liquid reagent tests for CO_2, one of which is an immersion CO_2 test that is installed in your aquarium and constantly reflects changes in the CO_2 level. This test is filled with a liquid reagent which must be replaced periodically, and it works by capturing a bubble of air under the surface of the aquarium water and measuring the CO_2 that diffuses as a gas into this bubble. The test does not give an actual amount, but changes color to reflect whether the CO_2 level is within the proper range for the water's hardness. This test is very convenient and highly recommended.

In a planted aquarium CO_2 levels are largely controlled by the rate of plant growth. If your plants are growing vigorously, they will extract more CO_2 from the water. The rate of plant growth is related to the amount of available light and nutrients. If you have provided proper fertilization and HID lighting, chances are that your aquarium will have a very high rate of CO_2 assimilation.

In most aquariums the CO_2 level stays within a

healthy range without the addition of CO_2, but some will require CO_2 injection for maximum plant growth. There are both simple and sophisticated systems for injecting CO_2 into the water, and the expense for these systems parallels their level of sophistication. A very simple CO_2 injection system consists of a bottle of slightly compressed CO_2 in an aerosol can, from which CO_2 is pumped into a plastic bell that remains submerged below the water surface. A bubble of CO_2 is maintained in this bell, and the CO_2 gas diffuses into the aquarium water. As the bubble shrinks it is necessary to pump more CO_2 manually from the aerosol can into the bell. This system is inexpensive and adequate for many applications, so long as the water hardness is kept within recommended levels. For planted aquariums lit with minimal fluorescent lighting, such a simple system is usually sufficient.

Aquariums lit by HID lighting may require more sophisticated CO_2 dispensing equipment. More sophisticated CO_2 injection systems consist of an electronic metering valve that dispenses CO_2 automatically from a pressurized canister according to the CO_2 readings as measured by a pH control. The control is an electronic device that constantly monitors the pH of the water and dispenses enough CO_2 to maintain the pH at a preset level. In this way more CO_2 is dispensed when the plants are extracting it, and less (or none) is dispensed when the plants are releasing CO_2 and consuming oxygen. The CO_2 is diffused into the aquarium through a flow reactor, in which water from the aquarium is drawn and mixed with CO_2 from the injection system. Such a system is highly efficient and effective, but is prohibitively expensive for many hobbyists.

Though this equipment is very effective and highly recommended, your commitment to it depends on the level of attainment with which you will be satisfied. If your are content with moderate plant growth and do not want to keep the most difficult species of plants, expensive CO_2 injection equipment may not be necessary. On the other hand, if you will be satisfied only by keeping the most challenging plants and having them grow and reproduce rapidly, more advanced equipment will probably be necessary.

Trace Elements

Certain trace elements must be added to the aquarium regularly because they are removed from the water by plants and chemical filtration, especially activated carbon.

Plants prefer to get their nitrogen as ammonium (see page 14), and there is certainly some ammonium in aquariums. Usually, however, nitrogen is present in aquariums as nitrate. Most plants can assimilate nitrogen through nitrate, but they must first reduce it to ammonium before the nitrogen is usable. Dense plant growth can significantly help reduce nitrate levels in the aquarium, but it is still necessary to regularly dilute the nitrate in aquarium water through partial water changes. Nitrate levels above 20 mg/L are stressful to discus, if not to other freshwater fish, and nitrate levels above 25 mg/L seem to be harmful to many more delicate, desirable aquarium plants such as *Cryptocorynes*.

Iron (Fe)

We know that iron is a very important nutrient for tropical aquarium plants. A constant level of .1 mg/L is about right for most tropical aquarium plants. Unfortunately, iron does not tend to stay in solution, so its presence in aquarium water must be constantly monitored and adjusted. Fortunately, accurate test kits and iron-rich fertilizers are available. A suggested level of .1 mg/L of iron may strike some as too low, but overdosage of iron is a source of several plant diseases, where leaves turn brownish-red and decay. A level of .1 mg/L has proved to be adequate for thriving growth of plants.

To maintain constant levels of iron without overdosing, an iron-rich liquid fertilizer must be added regularly, if not daily. This is because iron precipitates into an insoluble solid very quickly, and also because it is quickly absorbed by growing plants. Because each planted aquarium will consume iron at a different rate, depending on number of plants, intensity of lighting, and many other factors, the regularity and amount of the iron dosage must be determined by regular testing and evaluation.

Fertilizers can be added to the aquarium by hand measure or by automatic dosing pumps. Dispensing the fertilizer by hand is usually sufficient if it is done regularly, at least three times a week. By dispensing the fertilizer in regular controlled amounts you ensure that you will have neither toxic overdoses nor deficiencies of critical nutrients for the plants. As a convenient alternative, dosing pumps meter liquids in tiny amounts at set intervals.

Other Trace Elements and Water Changes

Though iron and carbon are the most significant nutrients for tropical water plants, they require many other nutrients that are called trace elements because they occur in minute quantities. Many trace elements are indispensible in tiny dosages, but would be toxic in larger doses. In addition, the proportion of nutrients (including trace elements) is as important as their presence. In other words, you can supply the proper amount of iron and carbon to a plant, but if a critical trace element is missing or depleted, plants will still not grow properly.

Unfortunately, it is difficult for the hobbyist to measure trace elements in aquarium water. Therefore, an intelligent program of water changes and fertilization is needed to ensure the presence of all necessary trace elements without toxic overdoses.

Trace elements enter the aquarium through substrate fertilization, tap water, and organic decomposition. A general broad spectrum aquarium plant fertilizer should be added to water when performing partial water changes. Do not continually add liquid fertilizer (other than the iron supplement) directly to the aquarium, because such uncontrolled fertilization will inevitably lead to overdoses of certain trace elements. By adding general fertilizers only to new water for partial water changes, you make sure

Typical Parameters of a Tropical Stream

Temperature	24.2°	C
Conductivity	20.2	µs
General Hardness	.13°	dH
pH	6.7	
Carbon Dioxide	9.0	
Bicarbonate	5.75	
Chloride	2.9	
Ammonium	.006	
Nitrate	0	
Phosphate	.028	
Oxygen	6.5	
Iron	.14	mg/L
Manganese	.15	
Calcium	.3	
Magnesium	.13	
Potassium	.9	
Sodium	2.5	
Sulphate	.48	

These are measurements of a typical tropical stream where aquatic plants such as *Cryptocorynes* grow in abundance. These measurements are provided for comparison purposes, but should not be interpreted as recommended nutrient levels for aquarium plants, as some of these nutrients vary greatly in nature.

that the new water is properly fertilized without overfertilizing the aquarium. If any buildup of a particular trace element occurs between water changes, the water change dilutes the buildup and solves the problem.

To avoid chronically overdosing nutrients, change a portion of the water often (at least 10 percent monthly) with hardness-corrected tap water. The new water should also be treated with a preparation designed to replace protective polymers and colloids that are present in the organically-rich water from which discus come. Tap water is harsh to the sensitive gill and skin tissues of fish, so we must add protective colloids to shield the fish.

The Planted Discus Aquarium

Suitable Plants for the Planted Discus Aquarium

Many common aquarium plants are not suitable for discus aquariums because of the higher water temperatures discus require. Feel free to experiment with other plants than those listed here, but watch them closely and remove them promptly if they appear to be dying. Rotting plants, or especially their roots, tubers, or crowns, can easily cause anaerobic conditions in the substrate. Consult a book on aquarium plants for more detailed information on the cultivation of specific species.

Aponogetons arc uscful as fast-growing plants for the newly planted discus aquarium, because they utilize nutrients stored in their bulbs, and thus can begin growing almost immediately after being placed in the aquarium. All *Aponogetons* "burn

Plants (1). Top Left: Vallisneria spiralis. Top Right: Vesicularia dubyana (Java Moss). Bottom Left: Microsorium pteropus (Java Fern). Bottom Right: Hygrophilia polysperma

out" quickly at high temperatures and require a dormant period at about 65°F (18.3°C).

Aponogeton undulatus, with its tall, narrow, wavy leaves, rapidly reaches a height of about 16 inches (41 cm), so it is useful for planting at the rear and the sides of the aquarium. It also propagates freely; a flower stem will develop "viviparous" plantlets that will eventually root themselves in the substrate. The aquarist may embed the plantlets, or remove them for relocation. If kept under sufficient light, *A. undulatus* may also develop tiny white blossoms.

Aponogeton ulvaceus develops leaves as long as 24 inches (61 cm), but the plant spreads out, so it is best placed in the center of the aquarium. The leaves are wider than *A. undulatus*, and the plant is among the easiest of aquarium plants to maintain. The double flower is an attractive yellow, and the seeds often germinate in the aquarium. Plan on this spectacular plant growing to a large size.

Aponogeton crispus is similar in appearance to *A. undulatus*, and equally hardy. It too produces a single flower stalk with white flowers from which seeds freely germinate.

Crinum thaianum, often called the "onion plant," is a hardy species that is a natural for the discus aquarium, because its leaves grow very tall—up to 5 feet (154 cm), and provide shade for the discus. A curtain of *C. thaianum* looks good across the back of the aquarium, and a dense group can provide a shaded retreat for the discus. This plant propagates profusely from a bulb, and small plants are likely to surround the parent plant. *Crinum natans*, a closely related species, is equally hardy and desirable.

Cryptocorynes are excellent aquarium plants. They are highly variable; several different species of "crypts" bear an array of leaves with many different heights, colors, and shapes. Crypts demand very good water quality, are particularly sensitive to nitrate and temperature fluctuations, and must not be continually moved and replanted. They prefer an iron-rich laterite substrate, but do well in standard aquarium gravel as long as the water is not too alkaline, since very alkaline water ties up trace elements. Most crypts also prefer moderate light levels, so it is a good idea to plant them around taller plants that will provide partial shade for them, particularly if HID lighting is used. Consistent nutrients must also be provided. Because of their demands, *Cryptocorynes* should be introduced into the aquarium only three months after other more hardy, faster-growing plants have been established. *Cryptocoryne affinis* is among the most hardy of the group. It will propagate readily, and has very attractive leaves that show well as a foreground plant, as it only reaches a height between six to twelve inches (15–30 cm). Its leaves are dark green on top with a reddish underside. Give *C. affinis* only moderate lighting. *Cryptocoryne balansae* is a taller plant—15 to 23 inches (38–59 cm)—with longer, bright green leaves with indentations, so it is suitable for background planting. Unlike many crypts, *C. balansae* needs lots of light, so plant it in the clear and allow it to shade other crypts. *Cryptocoryne ciliata* also needs bright light, and is a fairly easy species. It reproduces readily through runners, but because of its slender shape, plant it in a group of three or four plants. Other crypts may also work (*C. wendtii, blassii, griffithii*), depending on how warm you maintain your discus aquarium. All crypts grow relatively slowly and will not turn your aquarium into an unruly jungle.

Echinodorus sp. from South America are known as "sword plants." They are very attractive plants, and not demanding of water quality. Since they are marsh plants, however, they need substrate fertilization to thrive. *Echinodorus bleheri* is the large, well-known Amazon sword that deserves to be the centerpiece of the planted aquarium. Under proper conditions, this plant will grow large, so place it in a central location with plenty of open space; some pruning of inside leaves may be necessary. *E. bleheri* is very tolerant of hard water conditions. Its deep green leaves make an attractive display. *Echinodorus*

amazonicus, which requires softer water than *E. bleheri*, is often called the slender-leaved sword. This plant is smaller than *E. bleheri*, so is useful as a display in tanks where *E. bleheri* would be too large, or in larger aquariums planted in a group. The leaves are pale green. *Echinodorus cordifolius* is very different in appearance from its previously mentioned cousins, and is sometimes called the Radicans sword. It has very large egg-shaped or heart-shaped leaves, and requires bright light to thrive. Planting it in groups is useless because of its size and shape, but it does make a striking addition to the aquarium. Intense lighting is required to stimulate flowering. Aerial leaves are produced by a photoperiod exceeding ten hours a day; these should be pruned at their bases to encourage compact growth of the plant. *Echinodorus tenellus*, the pygmy chain sword, is appreciated for its tendency to form a dense carpet of greenery all over the

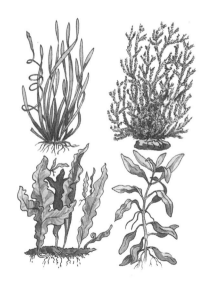

Plants (2). Top Left: Aponogeton undulatus. Top Right: Cryptocoryne affinis. Bottom Left: Echinodorus bleheri. Bottom Right: Echinodorus cordifolius

substrate. Varieties of *E. tenellus* are available that assume heights of between 4–8 inches (10–20 cm). Under bright light, *E. tenellus* will quickly sprout rhizoids bearing new plants. A foreground of *E. tenellus* creates a very desirable effect in a planted aquarium. If the pH is too high, or if the water is iron-poor, all *Echinodorus* sp. are apt to turn chlorotic (see page 56 on the plant ailment called chlorosis).

Vallisneria resemble large grasses, and should always be planted in groups. *V. spiralis* is the commonly seen larger val, and is tolerant of a wide range of water temperature and chemistry, but doesn't like overly soft water. It reproduces freely through runners, and female flowers possess a spiraled flower stem; hence the name spiralis. *V. spiralis* grows to a maximum height of 24 inches (61 cm). Some varieties of *V. spiralis* have twisted leaves, and are often confused with *Vallisneria asiatica*, the corkscrew val, or the *V. tortifolia*. The latter is differentiated from varieties of the taller *V. spiralis* by the maximum height of *V. tortifolia*, which is 8 inches (20 cm). Giant vallisnerian, *Vallisneria gigantea*, lives up to its name, reaching a maximum height of 80 inches (205 cm) in nature, but usually not more than 40 inches (102.5 cm) in aquariums, where the leaves bend over and float on the surface of the water. This effect is very useful for providing shaded areas for discus and *Cryptocorynes*.

Other suitable plants for the planted discus aquarium include *Vesicularia dubyana*, the Java moss, and *Microsorium pteropus*, the Java fern. Both of these plants should be attached with a rubber band or string to rocks or bogwood, not anchored in the substrate. Both of these plants are among the most tolerant aquarium plants. Java moss requires dimly lit areas, while Java fern tolerates brighter light. *Bolbitis heudelotii*, the African water fern, also does well in warmer water, and should also be attached to bogwood or rocks. It prefers subdued light, and is often slow to establish itself. The African water fern can be hard to locate in the trade. Another very attractive, though slow-growing plant is *Anubias nana*. Best as a foreground plant, it has small egg-shaped leaves of dark green. The floating plant duckweed (*Lemna minor*) is often condemned for the aquarium, but it is very useful as a provider of shade, and for preventing algae during the early days of a planted aquarium. Other useful floating plants that may be cultivated with varying degrees of success in the discus aquarium include *Limnobium laevigatum*, the Amazon frogbit, and *Salvinia auriculata*, the small-leafed salvinia.

Several species grow rapidly, and are appropriate for the newly planted aquarium, even if you don't like them and plan to remove them in favor of more desirable plants in the future. *Rotala* sp., such as *R. indica*, *R. rotundifolia*, and *R. macrandra* are attractive reddish plants that do well in a discus aquarium that is not kept above 84°F (28.8°C). Their beautiful color is maintained by intense lighting. Under moderate light they turn green, and under dim light they die. *Sagittaria* is another genus of plants that do well if the temperature is kept below 84°F (28.8°C), and the numerous species are useful for foreground, center, and rear planting. *Hygrophilia polysperma* is an easy plant that is undemanding and grows very rapidly.

There are quite a few other suitable plants, some of which are fairly inexpensive, so feel free to try others that attract you if their required temperature parameters are near those needed by your discus. Observe such plants closely, however, and remove them and their roots at the first sign of rot.

Common Plant Ailments

Upon discovering holes in the leaves of plants, you should first suspect damage by fish or snails. If you maintain any fish in your aquarium besides those we have recommended, observe carefully to see if they are nibbling on your plants. Snails almost always enter the aquarium on plants, and certain snails (if they are allowed to reproduce unchecked) can significantly damage plants. Usually, however, healthy, thriving plants survive such damage. Ramshorn snails (*Planorbis* sp.), however, can be of help in controlling algae if their numbers are kept in check. Avoid apple snails, which prefer leafy plants to algae. Insufficient light causes leaves to yellow and stems to grow weakly or not at all. Remedy the situation by cleaning the cover glass, by matching a more efficient reflector with your lamps, or by increasing the number or intensity of lamps. In deep aquariums (deeper than 24 inches [61 cm]), HID lighting may be necessary.

The wrong color spectrum will cause plants to grow tall and spindly or short and stunted. Lighting with too much red light (color temperatures lower than 4000°K) causes tall, weak growth, and too much blue light (color temperatures above 5800°K) causes short, stunted growth. Adjust the lighting to remedy the situation.

A deficiency in CO_2 causes plants to grow too slowly. White calcium deposits on leaves indicates biogenic decalcification of the water (see page 50), the condition of too little CO_2 in hard water conditions. Increase dissolved CO_2 by eliminating aeration with airstones, by increasing fish load, or by adding supplemental CO_2 to the aquarium water.

Trace element deficiencies of iron, manganese or potassium cause chlorosis, a condition where the veins of leaves stay green, but the intervein area becomes lighter green or yellow. This is because trace elements are not reaching the intervein area. Extreme deficiencies of iron cause the intervein area to look transparent or glassy. Remedy by increasing iron content of water to .1 mg/L with iron-rich liquid fertilizers or chelated iron products available from aquarium shops. Increase trace elements by more frequent water changes, by increasing the percentage of tap water (as opposed to deionized water) in the aquarium, or by addition of broad spectrum liquid fertilizers. Highly alkaline conditions bind up trace elements and encourage chlorosis.

An excess of phosphate causes blackening of leaves and plant death, as well as uncontrollable algae growth. Rectify by water changes with deionized water, as well as by including molecular adsorption resins in the filtration scheme.

Overdosage with iron causes leaf veins and then leaves to darken from brown to black, and to then deteriorate. If intervein area yellows but veins remain green, suspect not iron overdosage, but chlorosis caused by iron (or manganese or potassium) deficiency. Too much iron in the water causes phosphorous, an important plant nutrient, to precipitate out of solution as iron phosphate. Oversupply of iron can thus directly lead to deficiencies of phosphorous and manganese. Overdose of iron can also cause plants to expel manganese, so do not exceed the recommended dosage of .1 mg/L iron.

Nitrate excess causes the dreaded "*Cryptocoryne* rot," where the leaves of crypts blacken, patches of rot are eaten out of the leaves, and the plant quickly disintegrates. If the situation is remedied by water changes and filtration with molecular adsorption resins, the plants will often recover after being cleared of rotted tissue. If the outer, older leaves of a crypt turn black and fall apart shortly after being moved or introduced, or after light levels have been increased, the cause is more likely shock, and the plant will soon recover.

Suggested *Initial* Planting for a 75-Gallon (284 L) Aquarium

2	*Aponogeton crispus*
20–30	assorted *Hygrophilia* sp.
5	*Echinodorus bleheri*
15–20	*Rotala* sp.
30	assorted *Vallisneria* sp.
40	*Echinodorus tenellus*

Suggested quantities may surprise some, but these quantities are necessary 1) to consume the abundance of nutrients in a new aquarium to prevent algae and 2) to permeate the virgin substrate with oxygen via the plant roots.

The Planted Discus Aquarium

Occasionally an outbreak of "blue-green algae" overgrows and smothers aquarium plants. This so-called algae is really a cyanobacteria. It can be quickly eliminated by treating the aquarium with erythromyacin at 200 mg/gal. Expect some water cloudiness for a day or two during treatment, but after treatment the cyanobacteria will be completely eliminated.

Setting up the Planted Aquarium

A successful planted aquarium begins with careful planning. A planting plan should be drawn before the aquarium is filled with water. Based on your knowledge of which plants grow larger and which remain small, which do better in the rear of the aquarium and which are better suited to the foreground, draw a plan of your aquarium, taking into account terracing, driftwood, and rockwork. For diversity, you may wish to locate red plants next to green ones, and plants with large, round leaves next to plants with thin, elongated ones. Most plants will look best planted in groups. A plan will make things simpler and will prevent many problems.

Plant the aquarium according to your plan, removing snails and dead leaves and snails, and trimming long root growths to no longer than 2 inches (5 cm). It is wise to plant all the hardier, faster growing plants in large quantities. These would include *Rotala* sp., *Vallisneria* sp., *Sagittaria* sp., and *Hygrophilia* sp. Do not plant *Cryptocorynes* at this early stage! Plant the aquarium densely, not with just a few of each plant. Note the example of a suggested planting for a 75-gallon (284 L) aquarium.

After planting (a bigger job than you may think if you've never done it on this scale!), add water to full level, and treat the water with a general liquid fertilizer and a water conditioner. Turn on all filtration equipment. Connect timers, if any, to your lighting system, providing a 10–12 hour photoperiod. Take into account desired viewing times when setting the timers; that is, don't set the lights

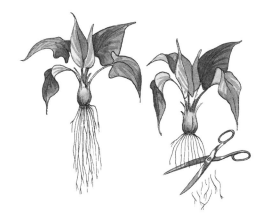

It is often necessary to clean and trim the roots of an aquarium plant before planting. Leave at least 2 inches of roots on the plant.

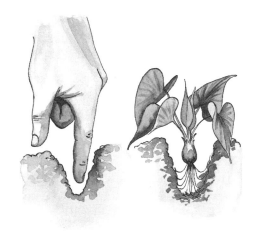

Use your finger to dig out a little cavity in the substrate, and place the plant upright in the hole.

The Planted Discus Aquarium

After filling the substrate in around the plant, pull it upward gently until the crown is visible above the substrate.

to turn off just as you arrive home from work in the evening! Put the thermometer in an easily visible place, and allow the next day or two for getting the water temperature adjusted. After the water has been filtered for a few hours, remove leaf fragments that have broken loose. The aquarium may still be quite turbid for another day or two. With a net, clear the water surface of any floating debris. Now you may want to put in a handful of duckweed, which reproduces rapidly, and is of immense value for discouraging algae by consuming nutrients. Additionally, duckweed turns yellow or brown and stops reproducing when starved for nutrients, so many experienced aquarists use duckweed to indicate when water changes and/or fertilization are needed. Overgrowth of duckweed can always be thinned by removing some of it by hand or with a net.

You should begin to see new plant growth within two to three days after initial planting. As soon as possible after planting, add your algae-control fish, withholding food for at least two weeks in order to encourage them to eat algae. Let the aquarium run through its conditioning period, which is very brief in a densely planted aquarium. Other fish may now be added.

After a month, making sure that the water temperature is within 82°F (27.7°C)–86°F (31°C), the aquarium is ready for discus. After three months, you may remove some of the redundant or less desirable plants and replace them with more delicate plants such as *Cryptocorynes*. Because discus are so easily "spooked," do this gently. It may be advisable not to add discus until after replanting.

This long discussion of the planted aquarium is just a synopsis of the needs and techniques of the planted aquarium. For more information and techniques, consult a good book on planted aquariums, such as Barron's *Water Plants in the Aquarium*, by Ines Scheurmann.

Suggested Initial Fish for Algae Control in a 75-Gallon Planted Aquarium

2　*Ancistrus* sp.
　　[bristlenose Plecostomus]
10　*Epalzeorhynchus siamensis*
　　[flying fox]
2　*Colisa lalia* [dwarf gourami]
2　*Jordanella flondae* [American flagfish]

The aquarium should not be fed for two to three weeks to force these fish to eat algae and nothing else.

Suggested Tankmates in the 75-Gallon Planted Discus Aquarium [in addition to the above fish]

Add these fish after ammonia and nitrite levels have fallen to zero, but before discus are added to the aquarium.

4–6　Congo tetras
8–12　emperor or cardinal tetras
pair　dwarf cichlids
pair　angelfish*

* Be especially careful to put these fish through the quarantine procedure before adding to the aquarium.

Nutrition and Feeding

The proper diet will produce healthy, thick, colorful, vital, disease-resistant discus. A proper diet is one that fulfills the nutritional requirements of the fish in a system that is easily managed by the average aquarist.

The Food of Discus in Nature

In their native waters, discus feed on insect larvae, small crustaceans, and assorted small worms. These foods are especially abundant during the rainy season when the water is rising and the discus are preparing to spawn. During the dry season, however, food sources are limited, and it is not unusual to find thin and emaciated discus in isolated bodies of water. In some areas (such as Lake Tefé), the dry season drives the fish out of moving water and into lakes, where food is more available. Incidentally, it is during this dry period that the highly-sought Tefé green discus are more easily caught, because the fish are more accessible in the lakes.

An often overlooked fact of nature is that fish do not live in havens of constantly abundant food. Even during the rainy season, when food sources are often abundant, different food organisms are available at different periods of time. For a few weeks the pupae of a certain insect may be available in droves, and the fish may consume these insects almost exclusively while they are available. During other times almost no food may be available, and the fish may go for weeks on minimal food. This is not to suggest that we should emulate this natural phenomenon in our aquariums, but it helps us realize that our discus are remarkably hardy and adaptable creatures.

Though discus consume mostly live food in nature, it is not necessary to feed live foods to discus in aquariums. In the past, aquarists went to great lengths to capture and cultivate live foods for their discus, but today there are many high quality prepared foods that are more than adequate for the needs of captive discus. In fact, live foods can introduce parasites and disease pathogens.

The Food of Discus in Aquariums

Prepared Foods

It is important to get your discus to feed on prepared foods as soon as possible, because prepared foods are dependable and easily available to the aquarist. Also, many prepared foods (unlike live foods) are manageable vehicles for vitamin preparations and medications.

Dry Food: Dry food is often available for discus in pelleted form. Pellets deliver a lot of energy in a small package, and discus easily accept a slowly sinking pellet. Many tank-raised discus, however, readily accept flake food floating on the surface because they have been conditioned to accept this convenient food by their breeders. You can get flake food under water by releasing it in the water stream from a filter or pump. Dry foods are excellent for discus, as they are enriched with vitamins and other essential nutrients, and they provide essential dietary roughage. The quality of dry foods has dramatically improved in the last few years, so a high-quality large flake or pelleted food is recommended. Dry tablets are also available, and these tablets can be pressed onto the side glass of the aquarium to give the fish easy access to the food. This tablet method is especially valuable when growing out a group of juvenile discus. The importance of dry foods for discus should not be underestimated.

Frozen: You can rely on frozen foods for a major portion of your fishes' diet. Commonly available frozen foods include bloodworms, beef heart, brine shrimp, daphnia, plankton, krill, mosquito larvae, black worms, and white worms, and mixed gel diets. While a varied diet is important for discus, the most useful of these frozen foods are bloodworms, beef heart, and brine shrimp. Beef heart is used by many discus keepers because it is relatively inexpensive, and because it can be used as a base for homemade blended foods. After cutting away all the fat (because solid animal fat can cause intestinal blockage), the beef heart can be mixed in a blender with beef liver, kidney, carrots, spinach, and unflavored gelatin for an excellent food. Beef heart can also be cut and fed in small wormlike strips. Beef heart, however, is not a balanced diet, and it contains thiaminase, an enzyme that destroys vitamin B_1, so beef heart should make up no more than 25 percent of the discus' diet. Frozen bloodworms are ideal, and are often useful in stimulating discus to spawn. Bloodworms are, however, more difficult for discus to digest than some other foods, so bloodworms should not be fed as an exclusive food source. Frozen bloodworms can be thawed in a squeeze bottle for easy feeding to a number of aquariums. Incidentally, frozen bloodworms are often called "red mosquito larvae." Frozen brine shrimp are the least expensive frozen food available, and though the brine shrimp possess relatively little intrinsic food value, their body tissues and exoskeleton promote digestion and help keep the intestinal tract clear. Avoid tubifex worms in any shape or form. Tubifex worms are generally collected in polluted water. Because of their tremendous disease-carrying capacity, tubifex worms should probably be called "typhoid worms."

Frozen mixed-gel diets are valuable for several reasons. They are blended, and provide your fish with a varied diet in one food source. Gel foods are also important because they are excellent for dispensing dissolved medications and vitamin preparations. If your fish are not accustomed to frozen gel foods, they will probably not accept a gel food laced with medication when they are sick. If taught to accept gel foods without hesitation, however, a sick discus will eat even if the food is laced with medication. Since often one of the first things a sick fish does is to stop eating, if you cannot get medication into a fish while it is still eating, more complicated treatments may be necessary.

Live Foods

Live foods are fine as a supplement to the discus' prepared diet, but they are generally unnecessary. It is true that live organisms contain impor-

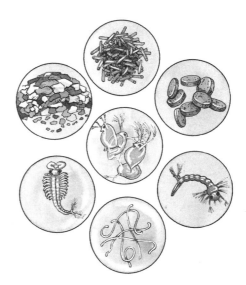

The foods of discus in aquariums. Center: water fleas (*Daphnia*). Clockwise from top: dry pellets, dry tablets, mosquito larvae, bloodworms, brine shrimp (*Artemia*), and dry flake food. All are useful foods, but none should be fed exclusively.

tant vitamins and other elements that the fish require, but most of these nutritional requirements have been duplicated in prepared foods. When conditioning a courting pair of fish, however, live food often serves to stimulate spawning. Live foods may also be necessary for wild-caught discus until prepared foods are accepted.

Live foods may be cultured at home, collected in nature, or purchased. If you choose to collect live foods, such as water fleas (*Cyclops* or *Daphnia*), be aware that live food may carry parasites. In general, because of the possibility of parasitic contamination, these live foods are not recommended.

Live brine shrimp (*Artemia*) are an excellent live food supplement for discus. They are a very clean live food source for which you need not worry about disease contamination. Brine shrimp may be hatched and grown at home, or you may purchase live brine shrimp at a retail store.

White worms (*Enchytraeus* sp.) are easily cultivated by the home hobbyist. White worms are too fatty to be fed as a major food source, but as a supplement they can be valuable. A starter culture can be purchased from some pet stores or more likely from specialty mail-order dealers. A Styrofoam box filled with moist potting soil and kept in the dark is all that is necessary to culture white worms. If the worms are fed with fish flake foods, they will be a very nutritious food source. Earthworms are also used as discus food. Note that if you feed earthworms, your fish may show mucous droppings from the earthworms that would not necessarily be an indication of disease.

Vitamins

A good aquarium vitamin preparation should be given to the fish regularly to eliminate the possibility of dietary deficiencies, particularly if no live foods are used. Instructions with liquid vitamin preparations often recommend adding the vitamins to the aquarium water, but since freshwater fish absorb little nutrition directly from the water, soak frozen foods in vitamins before feeding. Although the vitamins will be quickly washed out of the food, more of the vitamins may get to the fish. Gel foods can be thawed, soaked with vitamins, and then refrozen. Those health problems induced by environmental conditions (hole-in-the-head, etc.) often, but not always, show improvement when vitamin supplements are introduced into the food. Don't overdo vitamins: they are needed in minute amounts and can cause severe problems if overdosed.

The Feeding Schedule and Procedure

Because in nature discus are constantly foraging, in captivity many small feedings are better than a few large feedings. With only one large feeding per day, the fish still spends much of the day hungry, because the extra food quickly spoils.

The feeding schedule is usually limited by the work schedule of the hobbyist. Because most aquarists will be absent from the aquarium during daytime hours, an automatic feeder filled with pelleted discus food can dispense food twice or three times during the hours that you are gone. Besides these feedings, a morning feeding and one or two evening feedings add up to four to six small feedings a day. A feeding should consist of only as much food as the fish will entirely consume in five minutes. You do not want remaining uneaten food in the aquarium polluting the water and affecting its pH.

Feed at least two different types of food per day. An ideal feeding day might begin with frozen gel food (laced with vitamins) in the morning, two automatic pellet feedings during the day, a feeding of live brine shrimp in the evening, and another gel food feeding or frozen bloodworms a couple of hours later. Don't feed your fish within an hour of when the lights go out for the night, because the fish will quickly become inactive when the tank is darkened. A varied diet of clean, nourishing foods will go a long way toward ensuring the health and beauty of your discus.

Disease Recognition and Treatment

The main reason discus are considered difficult is their susceptibility to disease. Though keeping discus is not as difficult as many think, the fact remains that many aquarists have more disease problems with discus than with other common aquarium fish. Therefore, the discus keeper must surpass the average tropical fishkeeper in the skills of preventing, diagnosing, and treating diseases.

Methods for Preventing Disease

Obviously it is best to avoid disease rather than to have to cope with it, because many disease problems are difficult to diagnose, sometimes until it is too late, and some disease problems are difficult or impossible to treat at all. Proper disease prevention techniques will save you headache and heartbreak, because you can keep many diseases out of your aquarium in the first place if you follow a few rules.

Quarantine

All new fish, including discus and any fish intended to be kept with discus, should be in a three-week quarantine for disinfection and for observation. This is especially critical with wild-caught discus and those bred in the Far East. It is important that you observe new fish for signs of disease, and that you treat the new fish with preventive medication even if you do not see any signs of disease.

Many aquarists wish to keep other fish with discus, particularly those Amazon species that naturally occur with them, such as angelfish or corydoras catfish. However, many discus keepers believe that you cannot or should not keep any other fish with discus, because other fish bring disease problems to the discus aquarium. Corydoras catfish are notorious for carrying flukes and hexamita, while domestic angelfish are noted for carrying capillaria. While we do believe that discus are more susceptible to many diseases than these other fish, and that it is safer to keep discus by themselves, it is possible to mix other fish with discus if you follow a careful quarantine procedure.

A quarantine tank should be a part of every serious aquarist's equipment. We define quarantine as not just isolation and observation, but as isolation, observation, and preventive medication of all new specimens. The quarantine tank need not be large, but should be large enough to accommodate the largest quantity of fish you are likely to introduce to the main aquarium at any given time. Usually a 29-gallon (107 L) aquarium (L 30 inches [76 cm] x W 12 inches [30.7 cm] x H 18 inches [45.5 cm]) is sufficient to quarantine six to eight small discus or two to three adults. The aquarium should be outfitted sparsely, but with a large rock or two or a couple of clay flowerpots for fish to hide in. Light should be kept minimal, as bright light deactivates some medications. A full cover should be used, as newly introduced discus might jump out of an uncovered tank.

A sponge filter should be used for biological filtration, and a small box filter for mechanical filtration. The box filter is also helpful for removing medication after the quarantine period is over, when activated carbon can be put into it to adsorb medication from the water. Some medications destroy nitrifying bacteria; if those medications are used, temporarily remove the sponge filter, but do not place it in the main aquarium. A sponge filter from a quarantine tank could carry infectious organisms into an otherwise healthy aquarium.

Above left: A blue discus with fry clinging to its sides. ▶
Above right: Newly-hatched discus fry still clinging to the substrate on which the eggs were laid. Note that the eggs usually are laid on a vertical surface such as this one. These fry soon will begin to feed on the mucus secreted by their parents.
Below: A domestic discus, most likely a cross between a brown and a blue. This is a very young fish, as evidenced by the short ventral fins.

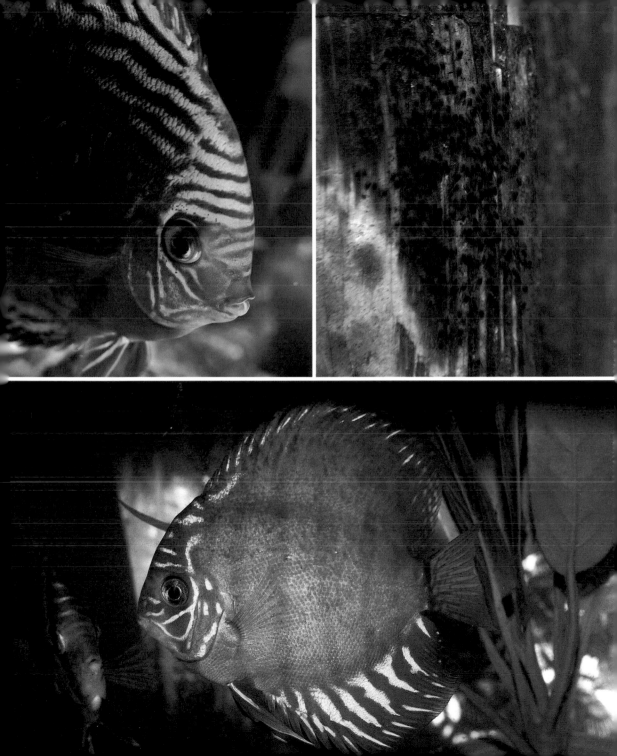

Disease Recognition and Treatment

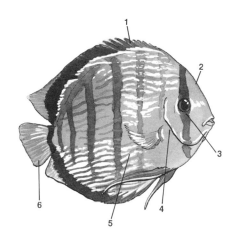

A healthy discus.
1. Fins in good condition.
2. Rounded forehead.
3. Clear eyes.
4. Gills in good condition.
5. Rounded belly.
6. Intact tail.

An extraordinarily ill discus. Fin and tail rot is evident, and fungus is growing on the diseased tissues of the dorsal fin. HLLE (Head and Lateral Line Erosion) is in advanced stages just above the eye. Bacterial lesions are present on the stomach area. Only a very negligent fishkeeper would let one of his charges get this bad, as such a fish is well nigh hopeless and should be euthanized.

The quarantine procedure begins with a medicated bath to remove any gill and body flukes that might be present. This medicated bath should be made of either praziquantel or dylox (see page 69). One bath is usually sufficient to rid the fish of flukes. After the bath, gradually acclimate the fish to the quarantine water temperature—around 86° F (30°C)—by floating the fish in the quarantine tank in a plastic bowl. After five minutes some water from the quarantine tank—approximately 25 percent of the estimated water in the bowl—should be gradually added to the bowl. Add this amount twice

during the acclimation process. This allows the discus to adjust gradually to the pH of the quarantine tank. After about 15 minutes, tip the bowl and release the discus into the quarantine tank. The lighting in the quarantine tank should be turned off for the rest of the day to allow the new discus to relax and get used to their temporary residence. Though discus are not normally shy of light, bright lighting will add to the stress of already stressed fish. Also, during the first week, nocturnal scavengers such as *Corydoras* sp., *Ancistrus* sp. and *Plecostomus* sp. should not be kept with discus, because these scavengers may frighten the discus and cause them to injure themselves by dashing about the tank.

During the first day or two of quarantine the fish should not be expected to eat, so begin with a very light feeding on the second or third day. Also, during the first three days the temperature of the quarantine tank should be gradually raised to 96°F

◀ Above: A red turquoise discus with early HLLE syndrome. At this stage, the disease can be treated easily.
Below: A green discus with more advanced HLLE syndrome.

Disease Recognition and Treatment

An aquarium set up for quarantine. The upturned flower pot provides shelter for stressed fish, and the heater maintains elevated temperature during the quarantine period. A sponge filter provides biological filtration, and a box filter contains filter floss for particulate filtration. If medication is used during quarantine, no activated carbon should be used in the box filter. Such an aquarium could also be used as a spawning tank, but the substrate would not be helpful.

(35.5°C). Warmer temperatures will accelerate the life-cycle of many parasites, speeding up treatment. Additionally, exposure to higher water temperatures helps eradicate two of the most common banes of discus, *Capillaria* and *Hexamita*. After the thirteenth day of quarantine—tenth day of 96°F (35.5°C) temperatures—the temperature should be lowered to 88°F (31°C). Note that *Corydoras* sp. catfish cannot endure temperatures above 92°F (33°C), so skip this part of the quarantine with those catfishes.

On the third, fifth, and seventh days of quarantine treat the tank with metronidazole at 250 mg/20 gallons (75.6 L). After each treatment (fourth, sixth, and eighth days) change 50 percent of the water. On the eighth or ninth day put activated carbon in the box filter to remove any remaining metronidazole. The metronidazole treatment will rid the fish of *Hexamita* and *Spironucleus* protozoans if present.

As soon as the fish begin feeding on a gel diet in quarantine, treat them for *Capillaria* and other

nematodes with fenbendazole. Dissolve the fenbendazole in the gel food 1 percent by food volume and refreeze. Feed this medicated food for one large feeding or two small ones. You should repeat this treatment again in three to four weeks to ensure that the fish are free of internal nematodes.

Ammonia and nitrite levels in the quarantine tank should be tested every other day. Water changes should be performed as needed to keep ammonia levels below .4 mg/L and nitrite levels below .2 mg/L. By the end of the three-week quarantine the fish should be free of the most common discus ailments and eating a normal aquarium diet, so they are ready to be transferred to the aquarium.

Good Water Quality

After quarantining new fish, the best thing you can do to prevent disease is to maintain consistently excellent water quality. Poor or fluctuating water quality puts fish under stress, and stress-weakened fish are not as able to fend off disease as are fish in a stable environment. It is critical to maintain ammonia and nitrite levels at zero, and nitrate below 40 ppm (ideally below 20 ppm). Though a particular pH and water hardness are not critical, it is important to maintain these parameters at constant levels. It is possible to maintain healthy discus at pH 7.5 and pH 5.5, but you will not be very successful if the pH in your aquarium constantly fluctuates between 7.5 and 5.5. Especially the temperature of the aquarium water should be kept absolutely stable at a temperature between 82 and 86°F (27.7–30°C). By weakening the fish, a quick temperature drop of 3° or 4° can bring on a parasite infestation.

Dissolved oxygen levels can be kept high by providing plenty of light for plants, by keeping mulm and accumulated wastes in the aquarium at a minimum, and by faithfully cleaning mechanical filtration media. As organics accumulate in the mechanical media, they decompose. Bacterial decomposition processes suck dissolved oxygen out of the water, and can cause consequential decreases in dissolved oxygen levels.

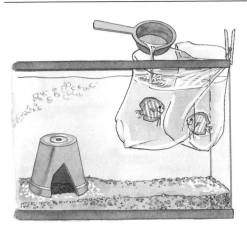

Acclimate new discus by first floating the bags in the receiving tank. This will allow the discus to gradually adjust to the water temperature of the receiving tank.

Open the bags immediately, but wait about 5 minutes before adding portions of water from the receiving tank to the fish bags. This will allow the discus to adjust to the water chemistry of the receiving tank.

Good Nutrition

Well-fed fish are usually healthy fish, and healthy fish are usually more disease resistant than unhealthy fish! If you are careful to feed your discus a varied diet, based on highly nutritious food, your fish will demonstrate much of their natural disease resistance.

You should get your discus to accept a gel-based frozen food as soon as possible, because gel-based foods are an excellent transport medium for medications. Because freshwater fish do not drink much fresh water or absorb it through their skin (as discussed earlier), medications are usually not efficiently administered dissolved in aquarium water. Therefore, it is often preferable to medicate fish through food. By medicating food you can better control the dosage the fish receives, because most of the medication gets inside the fish. Gel-based foods are convenient for carrying medications because they can be easily thawed, mixed with the appropriate amount of medication, and then refrozen. But if your discus have not been conditioned to take gel-based foods when they are healthy, they won't likely accept it when they are sick and "off their feed." Make a good gel-based food one of the three or four foods you regularly feed so you have this weapon in your arsenal when you need it.

Filtration Equipment

There are two more pieces of filtration equipment that can be immensely useful for preventing disease problems.

UV Sterilization: Ultraviolet sterilizers are used to kill bacteria and some free-swimming parasites in aquarium water.

UV sterilizers are very effective provided they are used properly. The flow rate through the sterilizer must be within a certain range. If water flows through the sterilizer too fast, its effectiveness is dramatically reduced. Follow the manufacturer's recommendations for flow rate through a UV sterilizer. The UV lamp must also be changed every four to six months. The band of UV light emitted by

Disease Recognition and Treatment

the sterilizer lamp is damaging to eyes, so you should never look directly at an unshielded lamp.

Ozone: The powerful oxidizing capacity of ozone makes it a potent agent against water-borne disease organisms. Ozone literally burns up bacteria, viruses, and many free-swimming parasites. Because it is such a powerful oxidizer, ozone should never be introduced directly into the aquarium. It should rather be used in some sort of an external reactor, where the ozone gas is mixed with water from the aquarium. This water should then be passed through activated carbon to remove any residual ozone before it gets back into the aquarium. Ozone is damaging to gill tissue, and is also damaging to the discus' sensitive skin.

Ozone and UV sterilization are somewhat redundant, so there is no need to use both methods for the same aquarium. Ozone is probably superior, in that it also is a means of chemical filtration through oxidation of dissolved organics, and because it also raises the dissolved oxygen content of the water. Ozonizers also do not require any regular service as do UV sterilizers. The serious discus keeper should consider using one of these methods for preventing disease.

We should also mention that diatom filters are able to filter many of the larger free-swimming parasites out of the water, so diatom filtration can be considered a mechanical aid in combating some parasite problems.

The Discus Keeper's Medicine Chest

Here are the medications you should keep on hand at all times and in sufficient quantities for those disease problems that typically plague discus. Note that several of these medications are available only from a veterinarian, so you won't find them at your local pet store. Most vets are happy (if not amused) to supply you with these medications when you explain your need. If you don't want to go to the trouble of getting medications from a vet, there is

Remember that if an antibiotic is working, you will soon see improvement. If you do not see improvement within the treatment period, chances are that the particular bacterium you are dealing with is not affected by the antibiotic (or that the problem is not bacterial), and you should try another antibiotic. Before changing antibiotics, however, do a 50 percent water change and filter the water through carbon for at least 12 hours.

usually an alternative treatment available from pet stores, but it will may not be as effective.

Note that you should discontinue all chemical filtration (activated carbon, resin pads, molecular adsorption resins, etc.) whenever medications are dispensed into the aquarium water. Also note that whenever you purchase a commercial medication from a pet store, you should follow the dosage directions for that particular preparation, even if they conflict with the dosages that follow here. This is because the concentration of the commercial preparation may not be the same as the pure medication mentioned in this chapter. Always be careful handling medications, and keep them in a safe place where children or pets cannot get to them. Mark all medications accurately, and store them with desiccants in a cool, dry, dark place.

Formalin/Malachite Green: Formalin is a 37 to 40 percent solution of formaldehyde gas in water, and malachite green is a dye. They can be used separately, but a mixed solution of formalin and malachite green has a synergistic effect (more effective than either medication alone) in controlling both external protozoans and monogenetic trematodes. Formalin is often used alone, as is malachite green, but malachite green (a carcinogen) has been shown to cause the same stress to fish at 1 ppm that formalin has at 100 ppm. Malachite green also stains the silicone in aquariums green, and malachite green is retained in the tissues of fish exposed to only .1 ppm. Thus, either formalin alone or the combination should be used. This combination is readily available as an over-the-counter preparation in tropical fish stores, though a breeder or large-scale hobbyist can make up a stock solution by adding 1.4 grams of malachite green to 380 cc of 37 percent formalin. Formalin is used in a one-hour bath at a dosage of 1 mL stock solution/gallon (3.8 L) (or 20 drops/gallon), or in an established aquarium at 1 mL stock solution/10 gallons (37.8 L) (2 drops/gallon) every three days for three total treatments. The one-hour formalin bath is excellent for body and gill flukes, and the three-day treatment is the treatment of choice for common protozoans such as *Costia*, *Chilodonella*, and other agents of "blue slime" disease. Malachite/formalin is the treatment of choice for "ick."

Formalin drastically reduces dissolved oxygen levels, so aeration must be provided via an airstone during the one-hour bath. Remembering that the capacity of water to hold dissolved oxygen decreases as the temperature increases, formalin should never be dosed into an aquarium if the water is above 80°F (26.6° C) without additional aeration. In addition, a one-hour formalin bath should never be used on fish with sores or ulcers, as the formalin will cause the fish to lose body fluids and dehydrate.

Dylox (Trichlorofon): Dylox is an organophosphate, available as an over-the-counter preparation under such names as LifeBearer, Dilox, Clout, and Masoten. This drug is effective against protozoa, gill and body flukes, and, to a lesser extent, *Capillaria*, but is highly stressful and potentially toxic to fish. Dylox treatment will make the fish nervous and will increase their respiration. Dylox, a neurotoxin, is very injurious to humans, and it is easily absorbed through the skin and mucous membranes, so you must be very careful not to inhale it or handle it without protective rubber gloves.

The quality of the dylox you use is critical. It must be a fresh, white powder. If the dylox is tan and clumpy, don't use it, because it has absorbed hu-

midity, and has become less active and more toxic. Fish are significantly more tolerant of fresh dylox than of stale supplies. Dylox should therefore be stored with a desiccant packet to absorb humidity. Dylox is very effective, but some strains of body fluke have developed a resistance to it, so its usefulness may vary. You therefore may find it better to use praziquantel instead.

Praziquantel: Praziquantel is available from veterinarians under the trade name Droncit. Flukes on wild-caught discus will be immediately killed by dylox, but tank-raised discus may carry flukes that have developed a resistance to dylox. Recent tests demonstrate that some flukes have developed a resistance to an amount of dylox above the lethal dosage for fish! Since, as mentioned, dylox is also very toxic to humans if breathed in or absorbed through the skin, praziquantel is to be recommended over dylox. Praziquantel is used in a one- to two-hour bath at a dosage of 15–20 ppm (mg/L) or 60–75 mg/gallon (3.8 L). It can also be dosed through food at 20–150 mg/kg (2.2 lbs.) of fish weight for nematodes (*Capillaria*). Praziquantel is very safe to use; overdosed fish display uncoordinated swimming and irregular breathing. Both symptoms disappear when returned to unmedicated water. Note that loaches display sensitivity to praziquantel, and should not be exposed to it.

Praziquantel is ineffective against fish lice (*Argulus*) and anchor worms, for which dylox is still necessary. Praziquantel also cannot be used in an aquarium with a functional biological filter, so use it only in a one- to two-hour bath or in food. Public aquariums routinely use praziquantel as an initial bath for both freshwater and marine fish.

Metronidazole: Metronidazole is available as the prescription drug Flagyl and in aquarium medications with the trade names Hexout and Hexamit. Metronidazole is used to treat the notorious internal flagellate protozoans *Hexamita* and *Spironucleus*.

Metronidazole is administered at 250 mg/20 gallons (75.6 L) every other day for three treatments, with 50 percent water changes in between.

The medication is absorbed through the gills and works systemically. As the fish improves, a food medicated with 1 percent metronidazole (1 gram per 4 ounces of food) should be given. The sugar base in metronidazole tablets may produce a bacterial bloom, so water changes every second day are recommended.

Fenbendazole: Fenbendazole is available through veterinarians under the trade name Panacur. It is very useful for *Capillaria* and other internal nematode worms. It is a very safe medication to use in either of two ways: either dissolved in a frozen gel food at 1 percent by food volume (1 gram per 4 ounces of food), or if the fish has stopped feeding, "tubed" with a syringe directly into the fish's mouth at 75–100 mg/kg (2.2 lbs) of the fish's weight (see page 71 for procedures for weighing fish). Panacur is most commonly available in a 10 percent suspension, so the above dosage should be multiplied by 10 when using a 10 percent diluted solution. One large medicated feeding or two small ones are sufficient to rid the fish of nematodes, but the fish should be treated again after three weeks. Often fish stop eating when infested with internal nematodes, so direct injection into the fish's mouth may be necessary. Ivermectin is also often recommended for internal nematodes, and is effective, but because the effective dose of ivermectin is dangerously close to the lethal dose for fish, fenbendazole is preferred. There is another drug, flubendazole, that is currently being tested for internal worms in fishes, but it cannot be recommended at the time of this writing because of a lack of data.

Potassium Permanganate: An old-fashioned cure, but still one of the best for external fungus, is potassium permanganate. A daily bath in a 1:5,000 dilution by weight—about 75 mg/gallon (3.8 L)—of these purple crystals in water is very effective against fungus. Always mix a fresh solution before use, as the solution quickly deactivates. The container used for the bath must be very clean, because potassium permanganate is an oxidizer and will be "used up" by organics in the container before the

solution can be effective against the fungus.

Sodium Chloride (Salt): Certainly the oldest medication for fish diseases is noniodized table salt. 1 tablespoon per gallon (3.8 L) of water will often cure mild cases of fungus in two or three days, and discus can handle the added salt for the brief time necessary. This level of salt will kill aquarium plants and most snails, hence a separate treatment aquarium is necessary.

Ceftazidine: Used by doctors under the trade name Tazicef, ceftazidine is extraordinarily effective for treating bacterial infections. Gaping, bloody wounds that are thought untreatable are often reduced to scar tissue several days after treatment with ceftazidine. Inconveniently, ceftazidine is generally used as an injection into the epaxial muscle just below the dorsal fin. The dosage is one injection, every third day for a total of three injections, at .1 mL of reconstituted solution per kilogram (2.2 lbs.) of body weight. Injecting medication into a fish might seem an unreasonable effort, but if an injection can save an adult discus from certain death, the bother seems a small price to pay. Ceftazidine is a relative newcomer to the aquarium scene, but its effectiveness borders on the miraculous to those of us who have for years watched precious fish die in just a few days from bacterial lesions. Ceftazidine is very expensive, so it usually is not used as a bath. Also, because ceftazidine deactivates rapidly after reconstitution, the unused solution should be frozen.

Nitrofurazone: Where ceftazidine cannot (or will not) be injected, nitrofurazone is the antibiotic of choice for most bacterial problems such as cloudy eyes, eroding fins and tails, external bacterial infections, and minor abrasions and wounds. Nitrofurazone does not inhibit nitrifying bacteria, so fish may be treated in the display aquarium if necessary. An additional benefit of nitrofurazone is that it may be safely triple-dosed in difficult cases. Nitrofurazone will color the water yellow during treatment, but this color will quickly disappear after filtering through activated carbon.

Disease Recognition and Treatment

Dissolve nitrofurazone in aquarium water at 50 mg/gallon (3.8 L) every other day for seven days (four treatments) with a 25 percent water change between dosages. The level of medication in the aquarium will build up over the course of the treatments despite the water changes. Nitrofurazone may also be added to food at 6 mg/4 ounces (.05 mg/gram) of food twice a day for nine days. If you find that nitrofurazone is ineffective against a particular bacterial problem, try a preparation of tetracycline according to its manufacturer's recommendations.

Furazolidone: An antibiotic closely related to nitrofurazone is furazolidone. It can be administered in food to fish at a dosage of .05 mg/gram of the fish's body weight for six days. This formula is based on the standard assumption that a fish eats 3 percent of its body weight daily. Obviously, it is necessary to weigh the fish (or estimate the fish's weight) to dose furazolidone through food. First, establish the fish's weight. It may be necessary to anesthetize the fish with MS222 to weigh it. Then find 3 percent of this weight. This is the amount of food to be medicated. Multiply this amount by 6 (days) to prepare a six-day treatment. Thaw the food and mix .3 mg (.05 mg x 6 days)/gram of the fish's weight into the food, and refreeze it.

Several commercial preparations are available that combine nitrofurazone and furazolidone. One such commercial medication is Furan II, and another is Furazone Light. A capsule of Furan II contains 60 mg nitrofurazone and 25 mg furazolidone. These combinations of nitrofurazone and furazolidone have been found to be extremely effective, and are highly recommended for bacterial problems. A simpler dosage is 250-mg to a pound of frozen food, fed once a day for six days.

MS222: MS222 is a tranquilizer (tricaine) used for shipping and handling of fish. It is dispensed in a dosage of 10 mg/L of water to ship fish, and 50–100 mg/L in a separate container to anesthetize fish for handling. MS222 is a humane way to relieve fish of stress if one must force-feed medications,

weigh the fish, or examine it closely. Another common anesthetic is quinaldine sulfate, but because fish are much more easily harmed by this drug, its use cannot be recommended.

Recognition and Treatment of Common Discus Ailments: Bacterial Problems

Fin and Tail Rot

Recognition: "Fin rot" designates highly contagious infections of the fins and tail by a number of bacterial agents including *Pseudomonas*, *Aeromonas*, and *Vibrio*. These are rod-shaped, gram-negative bacteria that usually infect tissues that have been damaged by poor water quality, injury, or as a secondary condition from a severe parasitic condition. The edges of the fins become cloudy and then white, and begin to fray. The fins then become reddish and inflamed, and the fish will finally succumb if untreated. With discus, fin rot usually occurs as a result of rough handling of wild-caught specimens, or because of too high pH that burns the fins and causes physical damage. In severe cases, fungus often attacks the dying tissue and complicates matters. In such cases, the fungus should be treated in conjunction with the antibiotic treatment.

Treatment: Fin rot is best prevented by maintaining good water quality. Water polluted with fish wastes encourages bacteria growth, and if enough infectious bacteria are in the water, they will find an opening somewhere in the fish's defenses.

Treatment of choice is with nitrofurazone or a combination of nitrofurazone and furazolidone. In very bad cases the dosage of these furan compounds may be doubled and tripled, or the fish may be put in a daily five- to ten- minute concentrated antibiotic bath containing up to ten times the normal dosage—up to 500 mg/gallon (3.8 L). If the nitrofurazone does not cause improvement in five days, use a tetracycline, kanamycin sulfate, or another broad spectrum antibiotic.

Disease Recognition and Treatment

Bacterial lesions

Recognition: Infected lesions often appear on fish. These are usually caused by *Vibrio* or other bacteria. The lesions appear first as a whitish patch on the skin with raised scales, but quickly become reddish and infected. Untreated, the lesion becomes a bloody cavity, which is soon infected by a variety of bacterial and fungal organisms. These problems are easily prevented by good aquarium maintenance, except in cases of traumatic wounds.

Treatment: Minor infections that have not progressed past the whitish stage may be treated by nitrofurazone alone. Severe cases should be treated by injection with ceftazidine, boosted by a moderate dose of nitrofurazone in the water.

Fungal Problems

Recognition: Aquarists who have never seen fungus often wonder what it looks like, and often mistake the whitish patches of an external bacterial or protozoan infection for fungus. External fungus (usually *Saprolegnia*) is a threadlike, easily visible cottony tuft. External fungus grows first on dead tissue, uneaten food, and dead fish eggs. Fungus is therefore a secondary condition of already diseased tissues. Fungus spores are present in aquarium water and multiply on uneaten food and accumulated debris, so a clean, well-filtered aquarium will have fewer fungus spores than a neglected or poorly managed aquarium.

Treatment: Fungus must be treated quickly because when the threadlike hyphae show up on the skin, the fungal filaments are ready to attack the internal organs. Mild cases can be treated with salt (NaCl, non-iodized) or potassium permanganate. Infected fish should always be isolated from other fish.

Protozoan Ailments

Hexamita

Recognition: This is the most dreaded disease of discus, but proper quarantine treatment for all new fish lessens the threat considerably. *Hexamita* are intestinal flagellated protozoa that attack the lower intestine. *Hexamita* infestations are often confused with a syndrome known as "Head and Lateral Line Erosion" (HLLE), which is caused by environmental conditions (see page 74). When infested by *Hexamita*, the fish often hide in the corner head down, become thinned at the head above the eyes, blacken in color, swim backwards, and excrete slimy white feces. The slimy, mucous feces are the first symptom of *Hexamita*, even while the fish are still eating and behaving normally. Every discus, angelfish, and *Corydoras* catfish could be carrying *Hexamita*, and should be given a prophylactic treatment in quarantine before being added to the display aquarium.

Treatment: Fortunately, a sure treatment for *Hexamita* has been validated by the experience of many aquarists. Metronidazole dissolved in aquarium water is sufficient for prophylaxis or for a minor case. More severe infestations are treated by feeding the fish with metronidazole dissolved in food (see page 00). In the most severe case the fish stops eating altogether, so the only way to get medication to the fish is by feeding a metronidazole solution to the fish through a tube. The fish is anesthetized with MS222 at 50–100 mg/L of water in a separate bucket so it can be handled with as little stress as possible. Dissolve 250 mg of metronidazole in a cup of water and take up some of this solution into a syringe. Liquid vitamins, powdered dry food, or frozen gel food can also be added to this mixture. Attach a short piece of thin plastic tubing to the syringe, and place the fish on a table wrapped in a damp towel. Through the feeding tube, feed the fish 1–3 mL of this solution daily for five days. After each treatment, allow the fish a few moments to swallow the solution, and return the fish to the tank. It is normal for the fish to expel some of the food upon its return to the aquarium. Note that because of intestinal damage, the fish may not begin eating for seven to ten days after elimination of *Hexamita*.

Disease Recognition and Treatment

Spironucleus

Spironucleus is similar to *Hexamita*, as is *Octomitus*, and it produces similar symptoms. For all practical purposes, the aquarist may consider *Spironucleus* and *Hexamita* as the same condition.

"Blue Slime" Diseases (Costia, Chilodonella, etc.)

Recognition: *Costia* and *Chilodonella* are parasites easily resisted by healthy fish. Weakened fish are susceptible, though, and show patches of excessive mucus, rapid breathing, lethargy, and then sloughing off of skin in patches. There is a gray coating on the body, often accompanied by bloody patches on the body. Fungus often follows.

Treatment: Formalin at 2 drops/gallon (3.8 L) every third day for three treatments is a fairly sure cure. Remember to add aeration whenever using formalin. Commercial preparations containing copper sulfate and trypaflavine are also available.

Parasitic Worms

Monogenetic Trematodes/ *Gyrodactylidea (Body Flukes)*

Monogenetic trematodes are parasitic worms that require no intermediate host, so they can rapidly multiply in an aquarium.

Recognition: Livebearing body flukes, *Gyrodactylus*, often attack discus. They reproduce rapidly, with each fluke containing within its body three more generations. The embryo within a mature fluke already contains within it another embryo, which already contains another embryo! A mature fluke can produce about a million descendants within a month. Body flukes feed on the skin and blood of fish. Each individual fluke does little damage, but massive populations are devastating to fish. Healthy fish in a healthy aquarium are usually able to resist serious damage. Flukes cause open skin wounds that become infected with bacteria, further compounding the problem. Worms removed

from the fish can live up to ten days without a host. Symptoms include twitching and scratching, but with the absence of white dots typical of "ick." In heavy infestations, minute red dots appear on body and fins, and fins may fray slightly.

Treatment: Praziquantel is the drug of choice, in a one- to two-hour bath. It is more effective than dylox and safer for the aquarist to handle. A dylox bath is often sufficient to eradicate body flukes from a fish, though some strains of body flukes are resistant to dylox. Retreatment in 14 days with praziquantel will eliminate any flukes that might have been present in the aquarium.

Monogenetic Trematodes/ *Dactylogyridea (Gill Flukes)*

Recognition: These are egg-laying gill flukes that can survive up to eight days without a host fish. Fish infested with gill flukes often breathe out of only one set of gills at a time. Discus with gill flukes also rub and scratch themselves against objects in the aquarium in an attempt to dislodge the flukes. In an attempt to expel the flukes, the afflicted discus often exhibit "spitting" behavior.

Treatment: A praziquantel bath is the treatment of choice for gill flukes. Since praziquantel eliminates both gill and body flukes safely, it should probably be used more often in place of dylox. If praziquantel is not available, gill flukes on wild-caught discus can be eradicated with a dylox bath.

Nematodes (*Capillaria*)

Recognition: *Capillaria* is introduced into the tank with wild-caught fish. Mild infestations are tolerated well by healthy fish, but a serious case emaciates the dorsal ridge, and then the rest of the body. The fish also becomes seclusive, and eventually stops eating. Often the stomach bulges with worms, not food. The infestation spreads as *Capillaria* eggs in a fish's feces are ingested by other fish. The eggs will not hatch outside of a fish, so good aquarium care goes a long way toward prevention.

Treatment: Every wild-caught discus, angelfish (*Pterophyllum* sp.), and *Corydoras* sp. catfish should be subjected to quarantine. During quarantine, and in case of any suspected infestation of *Capillaria*, fenbendazole dissolved in a frozen gel food is the treatment of choice. The fish should be retreated in 30 days to ensure total eradication. Praziquantel dissolved in food has also been used for *Capillaria* with mixed results.

Environmental Syndromes ("Hole in the Head")

Recognition: A source of great confusion among discus keepers has been the association of "hole in the head" disease with *Hexamita*. This stems from seeing both conditions simultaneously in the same fish, and from erosions around the head with flagellates present. These, however, have been nonparasitic flagellates that are normally present in the aquarium and that frequent diseased tissue. *Hexamita* has never been found to cause "hole in the head" disease, a condition that should now be called Head and Lateral Line Erosion (HLLE) syndrome, or cavitation. Fish with cavities and pits on the head and face have been dissected and have been found to have no intestinal flagellates. There have been cases of HLLE and *Hexamita* in the same fish, where the *Hexamita* was eliminated but the HLLE worsened. Conversely, HLLE has been cured by carrying out the following recommendations while the untreated *Hexamita* worsened.

HLLE begins as small pits on the head and face, usually just above the eye. If unchecked, HLLE causes cavitation on the head, with progressive erosion along the lateral line. Astonishingly, the fish lives through the syndrome, in some extreme cases appearing like a corpse while swimming around as if nothing is wrong. Eventually bacterial infections in the bared tissues lead to death. HLLE

is also often found in marine fishes, most notably in tangs and surgeon fishes (especially *Paracanthurus hepatus*), and juvenile angelfishes in the genera *Holocanthus* and *Pomacanthus*.

Treatment: HLLE is currently attributed to a nutritional deficiency of one or more of these essentials: vitamin C, D, calcium, and phosphorus. This deficiency is assumed to be the result of poor choice or variety in food, lack of partial water changes, or overfiltration with chemical media such as activated carbon. HLLE has been *reversed* by one or more of the following treatments: increasing frequency of partial water changes, adding vitamins to frozen foods, increasing the amount of flake food in the fish's diet (because flake food is vitamin enriched), adding greens as a food source (either fresh leaves or ground up in a frozen preparation), decreasing the amount of beef heart in the fish's diet (because beef heart lacks many critical nutrients), and removing activated carbon filtration. It is interesting to note that HLLE rarely occurs in planted aquariums, probably because fish gain nutritional benefit from nibbling on algae and plants, which are sources of vitamin C and other vital compounds.

Euthanasia

There are those cases when a fish does not respond to treatment, or a fish has acquired an untreatable illness, or a fish is so severely damaged or wounded that its death is inevitable. In such cases the fish can be placed in a sealed plastic container in enough water for it to stand upright, and this container is placed in a freezer, where the fish's metabolism simply slows down and stops. The humaneness of this method is demonstrated by the fact that the fish is found several hours later frozen upright, and not in a contorted position. Alternately, the fish can be given the anesthetic MS222 at 500 mg/L in a small bucket.

Breeding Discus

In the early days of discus keeping aquarists assumed that the life-cycle of discus must be similar to that of the related freshwater angelfish (both are in the family Cichlidae), and to which the discus was assumed to be related. In fact, early accounts in aquarium journals sometimes referred to discus as "blue angelfish." Aquarists deduced that discus would spawn under conditions similar to those of angelfish, and so they did. So aquarists removed the eggs from where the discus had attached them and put them in a separate aquarium, just as the aquarists did with angelfish, because angelfish were notorious for eating their young, and discus were too rare a commodity to allow the parents to eat their young. When the discus eggs hatched, however, the fry refused to eat anything presented to them, and they quickly starved to death. Not until it became known that discus young consume a special mucus on the skin of the parents was it possible to raise discus fry to maturity. Since this discovery, the discus' unusual way of feeding its fry has been one of its challenges and attractions.

A discus keeper who becomes interested in breeding has the opportunity to produce a strain with a unique fingerprint (i.e., color, pattern) whereby that breeder can be recognized worldwide. Most of us, however, have no such ambitions, and are happy to foster adult fish healthy enough to spawn, and to raise the fry to maturity. While the casual breeder may not be particularly interested in developing a strain of discus, all discus breeders should be careful to cull and breed selectively, so that the hobby is not debased with many discus of low quality. So much work has gone into developing the lovely strains of discus available today that it would be a crime to dilute them by indiscriminate breeding, though there are many excellent reasons to purposefully crossbreed one strain with another. An admirable goal would also be to preserve wild-caught strains, as these fishes have much to offer with their natural patterns and coloration.

It is not the intention of this book to be a comprehensive guide to discus breeding for the aspiring professional breeder. The subject of discus genetics and selective breeding alone would warrant a book, and it is the purpose of this book to be a comprehensive introductory guide for the discus hobbyist. If this brief section on breeding discus only whets your appetite, source materials are available from specialty societies and publications (see the appendix for bibliography and useful addresses).

Recognizing and Creating Mated Pairs

All of the discus species and varieties will hybridize among themselves in captivity, so it is important that you use discretion in putting sexually mature fish together. One can purchase already mated pairs, though they may not spawn after having been moved to your aquarium. Transport and change of scenery may alter the relationship, and they may even become extremely aggressive toward one another. If you do choose to purchase a mated pair, buy from someone you can trust, but understand that the seller cannot be held responsible if the pair does not spawn.

You can also buy a number of adult discus and wait for them to pair up. This is an expensive route, however, because you need at least six adult discus to "ensure" a mated pair. The best route, therefore, is to purchase a number of small discus and grow them to maturity.

It is a good idea to compose your discus population from several sources, or from different strains from the same breeder. This is because unrelieved inbreeding is often used to develop strains, and strongly inbred lines often produce stunted fish and fish with other problems. It is therefore usually best to pair discus from two different strains than to pair up two discus from the same strain. A population of eight to ten discus from three different sources is an excellent way to establish a variety of strains upon which to draw future breeding stock. Select your fish carefully according to the guidelines already given.

Breeding Discus

Adult fish displaying characteristic "pairing" behavior.

As the fish grow, you must develop an unflinching culling instinct. Superior fish will become apparent in time, and less desirable fish should be moved to other aquariums or given away. There is no reason to keep fish with inferior qualities unless these fit in with your private enjoyment of your aquarium. When you realize that you cannot possibly devote your attention to a hundred or so baby discus, you will preserve the best and cull the poorest.

Discus become sexually mature at 18 to 24 months, though healthy, well-fed fish may mature as early as 12 months. Pairing is indicated by constant proximity to each other, as well as by the fish approaching each other with heads tipped downward. Anal and dorsal fins darken, and the fish begin the twitching and shaking that is typical of spawning cichlids. Head and body coloration often changes, though the darkening of the dorsal and

anal fins is more noticeable. Typically the male will begin to clean a spawning site, which may be on plant leaves, a piece of pottery, or even the bare glass. Such behavior indicates that spawning is imminent.

Stimulating Spawning

It is easiest to stimulate spawning in fish that you have raised from juveniles, and it is hardest to stimulate spawning in wild-caught adult fish.

There are several techniques for stimulating discus to spawn, and these are usually performed in conjunction with each other. Discus will often spawn in hard, alkaline water, but if yours won't, try gradually softening the water with reverse osmosis water, rain water, or an ion exchanger. Raising the water temperature a few degrees to between 90°F and 92°F (32.2°C–33.3°C) helps, as does changing the diet to include more frozen bloodworms and a higher percentage of live and fresh food. Increasing the frequency of water changes is also helpful when you want the fish to spawn. A little extra effort on your part is appropriate, since you want the fish to exert a little extra!

Triggering a pair of discus to spawn can be as simple as performing a 30 percent water change with pure reverse osmosis water. This softening of the water simulates the softer water conditions created by the beginning of the rainy season in the tropics, which is the normal spawning season of discus.

Though discus will often readily spawn in hard, alkaline water, and hatched discus will develop in hard water, soft water is necessary for successful fertilization of eggs. If the total hardness of the water is much above 6°dH, the outer shells of the eggs will be prematurely hardened by the extra calcium in the water, and will be too hard for sperm to penetrate. It is also possible that sperm are immobilized by hard water. Of course, this will result in either no fertilized eggs or a very low hatch rate.

Breeding Discus

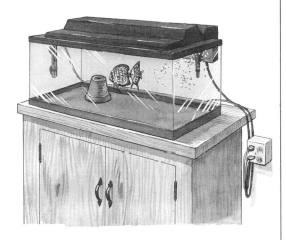

An aquarium set up for spawning. The upturned flower pot provides a clean, solid surface upon which the fish lay their eggs. No substrate is present, so the discus keeper can siphon up uneaten food, dead eggs, or dead larvae. SAFETY NOTE: Notice the drip loop in all electric cords leading from the water. Such a loop prevents moisture from running down the cord into the electric socket.

Before hatching, then, the conductivity of the water should be below 300 µs., pH around 6, and hardness no higher than 6°dH. Once the eggs have hatched, the young may be moved to harder water. In fact, some breeders believe that harder water helps prevent many disease problems that plague juvenile discus.

Hatching

A typical spawn is composed of between 200 and 400 eggs. Eggs are laid in a period of about an hour on the cleaned surface. The female lays the eggs in strings, and the male fertilizes them shortly thereafter—that is, if the fish is indeed a male. It is not unusual for two females to seem to "pair up," and only at spawning time does it become apparent that both fish are females. Even if the fish is a male, it still may refuse to fertilize the eggs. This does not

mean that the fish will never fertilize a spawn, but it may refuse for several spawnings. If the eggs are fertilized, the parents immediately begin to guard them against predators.

Sometimes a fish will eat its eggs shortly after laying them. This is, of course, frustrating for the aquarist, as an egg-eating fish is difficult to persuade otherwise. Sometimes pairing the fish with another mate ends the problem, and sometimes the fish stops eating eggs on its own after several spawnings. If a fish refuses to stop eating eggs after several spawnings, that fish should no longer be bred. Only those fish with strong parental instincts should be bred, so that destructive tendencies like egg-eating are not passed on.

The eggs hatch in about 60 hours. The eggs are constantly mouthed and fanned by the parents to keep them clean and oxygenated, and any dead or decaying eggs are removed. When the eggs hatch, the parents relocate the larvae nearby until the larvae are free-swimming. During this time the larvae get nourishment from their yolk sac. After 50–70 hours the larvae search out and hover near their parents' sides, where they scrape off bits of mucus for nourishment for five or six days. Persistence is necessary for the larvae, as frequently the parents avoid the larvae for a while, seemingly irritated at their presence. Persistence usually pays off, however, and the young are accepted by their parents. The parents take turns with each other during the feeding process.

After four or five days the young begin to make brief excursions away from their parents. At this time the young will begin to accept newly hatched brine shrimp as food. Baby brine shrimp should be fed three times a day until the young fish have been entirely weaned from their parents.

Rearing Young Discus

There are two methods of raising the young discus: the natural method, and the "artificial" method. Most discus breeders allow the fish parents

Breeding Discus

After hatching, the larval discus feed upon a mucus secreted by the parents. During this time the babies constantly swarm around the parent.

to raise their own young. Others, fearful of discus parents' eating or neglecting their young, have taken to removing young discus from their parents immediately after hatching and raising them "artificially" on a dried egg mixture.

The artificial method involves making a paste out of a dried egg mixture, which is smeared on the inside edge of a small container. The fry are moved into this small container, where they feed on the egg mixture as they would on the mucus from the side of their parent. Sometimes pulverized powder made from flake food, mixed with dried egg powder or used alone, is also used for larvae. The fry must be moved back into their holding tank before the water is fouled from the egg mixture, and then the small feeding container must be cleaned and refilled to be ready for the next feeding two hours later. An airstone should be placed in the feeding container while the fry are there, and they should be observed during the feeding process to make sure they are not stressed from too much pollution from the egg mixture.

If the aquarist is willing to undertake it, the artificial method yields a higher success rate. Fertilized eggs will be hatched and raised without risk of being eaten or neglected by their parents. The artificial method is virtually a full-time job. The fry must be fed every few hours, and because dried egg pollutes water virulently, the water must constantly be changed and fry moved from small feeding container back to holding tank, and back to small feeding container a few hours later. Discus that have been raised on this method demonstrate no appreciable differences from those that were raised by their parents.

The main objection to the artificial method is that it might intensify the very problem it was designed to combat: parental neglect. In nature, the genes of neglectful parents are not inherited, because neglected or eaten young don't live to spawn. In this way, if parenting instincts are genetic, "good parenting" is naturally selected in, and "bad parenting" is selected out. This is the natural process whereby a species' weaknesses tend to be bred out, and its strengths are reinforced. The artificial method of raising discus fry defeats this natural selection, and possibly encourages the propagation of discus strains that might be neglectful parents. If the artificial method of discus rearing gains wide acceptance, we might soon have numerous discus that *must* be raised artificially, and this will be a sad day for the nonprofessional discus breeder.

Why is this such a big deal? Well, why do we keep discus, after all? Do we not keep discus at least partly because we wish to observe the natural behaviors of fish in our homes? And isn't the unusual method whereby discus rear their young one of their most fascinating qualities? What a loss it would be if the average home hobbyist never had the chance to observe his discus successfully tending their young.

Index

Color photos are indicated in **boldface**.

79

Index

Useful Literature and Addresses

Books

Andrews, Dr. Chris, Exell, Adrian, and Carrington, Dr. Neville, *The Manual of Fish Health.* Morris Plains, NJ: Tetra Press, 1988.

Carrington, Dr. Neville, *A Fishkeeper's Guide to Maintaining a Healthy Aquarium.* London: Salamander Books, 1985.

Herwig, Nelson, *Handbook of Drugs and Chemicals Used in the Treatment of Fish Diseases.* Springfield, IL: Charles C. Thomas Publishers.

Roberts, Dr. Ronald, ed., *Fish Pathology.* London: Bailliere Tindall.

Scheurmann, Ines, *The New Aquarium Handbook.* Hauppauge, NY: Barron's, 1986.

————, *Water Plants in the Aquarium.* Hauppauge, NY: Barron's, 1987.

Addresses

Aquarium Fish Magazine
  P.O. Box 6050
  Mission Viejo, CA 92693
Journal of Aquariculture and Aquatic Sciences
  7601 E. Forest Lakes Dr. NW
  Parkville, MO 64152
The Discus Study Group
  7347 184 St.
  Fresh Meadows, NY 11366